A FORGE OF
FREEDOM BOOK

The Thirteen Colonies
1763

THE
SOUTH
CAROLINA
COLONY

by

Marguerite Couturier Steedman

CROWELL-COLLIER PRESS
Collier-Macmillan Limited, London

To the bright memory of Nancy Stewart
To the dear loyalty of Elswyth Thane

Library of Congress Catalog Card Number: 74–95299

The Macmillan Company
866 Third Avenue
New York, New York 10022
Collier-Macmillan Canada Ltd., Toronto, Ontario

Printed in the United States of America

FIRST PRINTING

PICTURE CREDITS

Photographs by author, 87, 106; B&B Studios, 82, 85; Gibbes
Art Gallery Collection, 52, 56, 110; Charleston Trident
Chamber of Commerce, 5; From the Colonial Williamsburg
Collection, 46–47; Culver Pictures, Inc., 3, 25, 35, 72,
98; T.C. Johnson, 90–91; Historical Pictures Service—Chi-
cago, 22, 30, 38, 55, 61, 69, 77, 97; McKissick Collection,
South Caroliniana Library of University of South Carolina,
10, 16; South Caroliniana Library of University of South
Carolina, 119.

JACKET ILLUSTRATION: *Settlers landing in South Carolina.*

Acknowledgments

The author wishes to offer her warmest thanks to the following organizations and individuals who gave invaluable help in gathering information and illustrations for this book.

Miss Virginia Rugheimer and the staff of the Charleston Library Society who let me have books for long periods and offered advice on sources of information which were extremely helpful. The reference librarians of the Charleston County Library answered a great number of telephone questions with speed and great courtesy. Mrs. Granville T. Prior, director of the South Carolina Historical Society and her experienced staff aided greatly in research, as did Dr. Milby Burton, director of the Charleston Museum and Mrs. Robert Hartzog, its Membership and Public Relations Director. I owe them many thanks for aid in research and for permission to photograph exhibits in the museum and in its Heyward-Washington House museum.

Miss Helen G. McCormack, Curator of the Gibbes Art Gallery Collections, secured for the book the reproductions of portraits of Maj. Gen. William Moultrie, Sir Nathaniel Johnson, and Col. William Rhett. The Tourist and Travel Development Department of the Charleston Trident

Chamber of Commerce gave the picture of the giant live oak used in the book.

Warm thanks are due the South Caroliniana Library of the University of South Carolina, whose staff, when asked if certain rare pictures and drawings were in their collection, would reply, "Yes, and we are having eight-by-ten glossy prints made for you!" Mr. Frank Coleman, Co-Director of the Walnut Grove Plantation Museum, near Spartanburg, S.C., graciously furnished photographs of this fine restoration of an Up-Country home and permission to reproduce them. Colonial Williamsburg furnished without charge the view of Charles Town before 1739. Mr. Marion W. Culp, Director of Information and Publications, Travel Division, South Carolina Department of Parks, Recreation, and Tourism, sent much information on historic sites in the state, and photographs.

The author is also grateful to the National Society of the Colonial Dames of America in the State of South Carolina, who allowed the author to photograph their property, the Powder Magazine, Charleston's oldest public building.

Elswyth Thane Beebe, a friend of many years' standing, gave priceless encouragement and considerable impetus to the writing. Alberta Lachicotte Quattlebaum of Georgetown and Mt. Pleasant, S.C., loaned the author books from her library, answered endless questions on rice culture and, as friend and neighbor, suffered with the writer through many versions of the manuscript.

Contents

The South Carolina Colony

 *Spain and the New World*

In 1970, South Carolina celebrated her 300th birthday.

Early in April, 1670, a nameless sloop and a battered frigate, the *Carolina* landed about 148 English settlers on high ground some three miles up the Ashley River, near modern Charleston, after a nightmare voyage. Four other settlements made by Spain in Carolina, and one attempted by France, had failed. This one just might succeed.

The story of South Carolina begins with Spain's conquest of the New World. The first European colony on the eastern shores of North America had been made at Winyah Bay, near modern Georgetown. Here, in 1526, a wealthy Spanish official, Lucas Vásquez de Ayllón, landed six shiploads of settlers, slaves, supplies, and livestock on land already claimed for Spain by a captain sent out by de Ayllón five years before, to explore the Carolina coast.

Ever since Columbus, sailing under the Spanish flag, had discovered the islands he thought were part of Asia, Spain had claimed most of the western world. Her explorers had planted flags or carved crosses on trees, marking the land as property of Their Majesties, Ferdinand and Isabella, or of their grandson, Charles V, king of Spain and emperor of the Holy Roman Empire, the most powerful combination of countries in Europe.

In the western world, another empire, New Spain, was rising. By the time the first Spanish colony was founded in Carolina, the islands of the Caribbean—Hispaniola (now divided between Haiti and the Dominican Republic), Cuba, and the rest were completely Spanish. Shortly, Spain's explorers had crossed the Caribbean to Mexico and Yucatán, fantastic lands of great stone cities, temple-pyramids rising above the jungle and unbelievable treasures of gold, silver, and jewels. For a century, Spain looted these, sending home literally tons of silver and gold aboard the "Silver Fleet" convoyed by warships. No wonder adventurers came across the sea in search of instant wealth. Their feelings were expressed by Bernal Díaz del Castillo, a soldier-adventurer serving under Hernando Cortés, conqueror of Mexico, "We came here to serve God and the king, and to get rich."

Though some gold had been found in the West Indies, their real wealth lay in the sugar cane fields that soon spread across the islands. The Indians, who had hunted in the tropical forests, fished when they liked, gardened when they must, were herded into dark mines or out into the broiling sun of the cane fields. Ill-fed and cruelly treated, they died by the thousands.

To replace this vanishing supply of labor, Spain began importing African slaves which had been captured in tribal wars and sold to Portuguese traders who shipped them from West African ports. There, European captains loaded them on ships bound for Europe and the New World. Often, the helpless prisoners were packed so tightly below decks that many died at sea. (Old captains declared they could smell

Charles V, king of Spain and emperor of the Holy Roman Empire

a slave ship three miles away!) The distance these slaves had to be carried and their high death rate on the voyages made them rather expensive. West Indian planters found it cheaper to capture Indians, if any could still be found.

This Indian slave-trade played an important part in South Carolina history. It was Francisco Gordillo, a Spanish discoverer turned slave hunter, who first explored the Carolina coast and brought back news of its wealth and beauty to Hispaniola.

Gordillo's employer, Lucas Vásquez de Ayllón, was a wealthy and (for that time) kind-hearted official on Hispaniola. Though he owned Indian slaves, he disapproved of capturing more of them. De Ayllón had heard rumors of a vast, rich, unknown land north of Florida, which was then thought to be an island. In 1520, he sent Gordillo to explore the Atlantic coast as far northward as possible. De Ayllón made his captain promise not to capture any natives.

Gordillo sailed northward for many months, landing occasionally to get food and water, explore the country, and carve crosses on trees. Like other explorers, he had to make his maps as he went, for the ones he had showed only blanks beyond the coastlines. His navigation instruments were few and primitive. From his confused descriptions, we cannot tell whether he reached what is now New York or turned southward near Virginia.

We do know that on August 18, 1520, Gordillo touched an island which he named Santa Elena (Saint Helena) and entered what is now Port Royal Sound. Even if he had sailed no farther north than Virginia, no Spaniard had travelled so far up the Atlantic coast as Gordillo had done. His voyage confirmed Spain's claim to the whole Atlantic coast as far north as Newfoundland. This vast territory was called "Florida."

In 1521, Gordillo, turning south, met another ship whose captain, Pedro de Quexós, was slave-hunting for markets in the West Indies. Quexós persuaded Gordillo to join the slave-hunt and divide the profits. Continuing south, the two ships dropped anchor at the present Pawley's Island, near modern Georgetown. Twenty men went ashore.

The beach was swarming with excited natives, pointing in wonder at the big caravels riding high in the water, with their brightly painted sails and their carved, gilded woodwork. The Indians stared at the bearded Spaniards' colorful clothing and shining steel helmets and breastplates, and then fled. The white men followed and caught a man and a woman. Rowing them out to the ships, they loaded them with presents, dressed them in Spanish clothing, and returned them to shore. It was not long before the whole tribe was back on the beach. The Spaniards gave them presents, too.

The kind of oaks the Spaniards found

While this friendly powwow was going on, the caravels sailed upstream into what is now Winyah Bay. Here they anchored. The chief of the neighboring tribe came out to the ships with his men, paddling long, dugout canoes. They brought gifts of food, furs, small pearls, and some silver. The chief offered guides to help the white men explore the country. Its name, he said, was Chicora.

The Spaniards marched through the woods thick with magnificent pine trees, some ninety feet tall. They noted the spreading live oaks with limbs as large and often as long as ordinary trees are thick and tall. Cypress grew in the swampy places. The woods were full of game. Fish leaped in the river. The soil was black, fertile.

On June 21, 1521, Gordillo and Quexós carved crosses on the trees, claiming Chicora for Charles V. That day, they invited all the Indians to the ships, for a feast. While everybody was laughing and eating, up came the anchors, the big, painted sails were spread and the caravels carried the natives of Chicora off to Hispaniola—and slavery.

This mass kidnapping of one hundred forty peaceful, trusting people had its effect on the early history of South Carolina, Georgia, and Florida. Word spread among the natives that no white man could be trusted. Pietro Martiri d'Anghiera (better known as Peter Martyr), a learned Italian living at the Spanish court, wrote, "So, throughout the whole country, they left enemies where there had been friends; and a peaceful land in turmoil, since children had been snatched from parents and husbands from wives."

De Ayllón was furious with Gordillo. He appealed to the governor of Hispaniola, Diego Columbus, son of the Discoverer, who ordered the Indians freed and cared for until they could be returned to their homeland. De Ayllón kept several of them. He became especially fond of one man, had him baptized a Christian, and named him Francisco Chicora. Francisco quickly learned Spanish. What he told de Ayllón, together with the reports of Gordillo and Quexós, made de Ayllón hurry to Spain. There he would ask the emperor's permission to found a colony in the rich, unknown country of Chicora and be its governor.

chapter two

The Coming of the Spaniards and the French

On June 12, 1523, Charles V granted de Ayllón permission to explore and colonize Chicora and neighboring lands—at his own expense. By mid-July, 1526, de Ayllón had spent most of his fortune to buy and equip six ships and pay the expenses of 500 settlers and many Negro slaves, several priests, a druggist, and several doctors.

After one unsuccessful landing, the Spaniards finally reached Winyah Bay, into which five rivers flow. The natives called the largest one Waccamaw. De Ayllón named it Gualdape. On a narrow neck of land between river and ocean, the settlement of San Miguel de Gualdape began.

The colonists had landed in August, perhaps the hottest month in South Carolina. The sun beat down from midmorning until late afternoon, making work in those hours almost impossible. The rich, black soil was a tangle of roots that fought the settlers' hoes, spades, and axes.

Swarms of gnats, deerflies, and mosquitoes tormented the

white men. Chiggers and ticks dug into flesh, causing unbearable itching and sores. Rattlesnakes, copperheads, water
moccasins, and the beautiful coral snake, deadly as its cobra
cousin, were constant dangers. Alligators, wildcats, panth-
ers, bears, and wolves must have eaten many of de Ayllón's
cattle and sheep.

The settlement would follow the same plan as others, for
the next one hundred fifty years. A stout palisade of sharpened logs protected the storehouse where food, powder, and
supplies must be kept safe and dry. Houses were built last
of all.

Nobody should have gone hungry here. The surrounding
waters swarmed with fish. Huge piles of oyster shells left
by the Indians showed how easily more shell fish could be
found. Great flocks of doves, wild ducks, and geese flew overhead. Wide, zigzag tracks left by sea turtles on the beaches
led to scarred, flattened sand heaps covering round, soft-
shelled eggs—sometimes fifty to one nest.

Fat squirrels, rabbits, deer, wild turkeys roamed the forests. Grapevines hung with fruit twined the tree trunks.
Blackberries grew in the sunny places. In late summer,
thickets of wild plum and peach trees were heavy with
fruit. Hickory nuts, chinquapins—little wild chestnuts—
were there for the gathering. One wonders why settlers
often starved to death, once they could get no more food
from the Indians.

Not starvation but malaria wiped out most of this settlement. One of the first to die was de Ayllón, on October
18, 1526. Winter was approaching, men were still dying,
and the colonists decided to return to Hispaniola. At sea,
a blizzard struck the ships. Men who had survived fever,
hunger, and hardship froze to death below decks. Of the
five hundred settlers who had sailed for Carolina, fewer than
sixty reached home.

In 1537, Charles V granted de Ayllón's vacant Chicora

lands to Hernando de Soto, the newly appointed governor of Cuba. De Soto's expedition of nine ships and more than six hundred men sailed from Havana in May, 1539, and landed at Tampa Bay. De Soto's zigzag march of discovery lasted four years. To the Indians of Florida, Georgia, the Carolinas, Tennessee, Alabama, and Mississippi, it was a nightmare. In friendship, they met him with gifts of food, furs, and pearls, offering themselves as guides. He repaid them by enslaving hundreds.

Wounded, lost, weary, seeking treasures they never found, the Spaniards crossed Alabama and followed the Alabama River down to Mobile Bay. Turning northwest, de Soto marched on, to discover the Mississippi River in 1541 and to die of fever on its banks. The survivors floated down to the Gulf of Mexico in crude boats and somehow returned to Cuba.

France, too, tried to settle Carolina.

Throughout the sixteenth century Europe had been torn by religious struggles. Catholics fought Protestants as traitors to the Christian faith. Protestants battled Catholics for the right to worship God as they chose. Nowhere was the struggle more bitter than in France, where *eight* civil wars, with few truces, lasted from 1562 to 1598. Throughout the war-torn land, the French Protestants, or Huguenots, were deciding to go somewhere that would give them peace and freedom.

In 1562, Jean Ribault, a Huguenot officer in the French navy, sailed with five ships and 150 settlers into Port Royal Sound. Friendly Indians greeted them with gifts—palm leaf baskets, pearls, deerskins, balls of cotton. Ribault's men had strict orders to trade honestly with the natives and treat them courteously. This kindness of the French was never forgotten. The Indians treated them like members of their own families. They even learned Huguenot hymns which they sang to later explorers.

Prom Lupi

Portus Regalis, siue F. S. Helenæ

Jacques LeMoyne's painting of the French arriving at Port Royal

On what is now Parris Island, near Port Royal, Ribault's men built a small fort, calling it Charlesfort, in honor of their king. Leaving thirty men in Carolina, Ribault sailed for France, on June 11, 1562, promising to return quickly with more settlers and supplies. While he was gone, however, the settlers went gold hunting instead of planting crops. When the outbreak of another civil war kept Ribault from coming back, the starving settlers fought among themselves and finally decided to return to France. In a tiny ship, its sails made of sheets and shirts, the refugees headed home. Weeks later, an English ship rescued them, half-mad with hunger, thirst, and terror.

When Philip II of Spain heard of the French settlement at Charlesfort, he was furious. He sent his most brilliant and merciless commander, Pedro Menéndez de Avilés to wipe out any remaining Frenchmen and prevent future settlements. Menéndez, with nineteen ships and 1,500 soldiers, found a second French colony, headed by Ribault's lieutenant René de Laudonnière, on the banks of the St. John's River in Florida. A bloody battle, ending in a massacre of Huguenot prisoners, followed. Then the Spaniards began building a chain of forts along the Atlantic coast from Florida as far north as Port Royal.

On August 28, 1565, Menéndez laid the foundations of what later would be the great fortress of St. Augustine. On the site of Charlesfort, Menéndez completed, in just sixteen days, the fort and town of San Filipe. In 1576, the Indians burned San Filipe, but Menéndez built another fort, San Marcos, near by.

Thus, France's first attempt to colonize the eastern coast of North America not only failed, but led to the founding of more Spanish strongholds.

Wars in Europe, Indian attacks, troubles within Spain itself and English attacks on Spanish settlements in Central America and on the Silver Fleet were all loosening Spain's grip on the New World. In 1586, Philip II was forced to order San Marcos abandoned.

France, however, would return to Carolina, not in colonies but in the small bands of Huguenots who would take refuge among the English settlers, a century later. Their fine minds, skilful hands, honesty, independence, and devotion to duty would leave a shining mark on the life of the province which endures to this day.

chapter three

 *The Indians of Carolina*

From 1586, when Spain abandoned San Marcos, until 1663, when English explorers touched the Carolina shores, the Indians had their beautiful country to themselves. Between tribal wars, they went on building their towns, fishing, and tending gardens and corn patches with hoes of conch shell or sharpened stone. They glided down their rivers in the same sort of dugout canoes their fathers had made. It was as though the white man had never come.

Some twenty-five or thirty tribes made their homes wholly or partly in what is now South Carolina. They were members of five great Indian stocks or divisions—the Iroquoian, Siouan, Muskhogean, Algonkin, and Yuchi people who, with others, inhabited the North American continent. Their territories reached from the high, densely wooded peaks of the Blue Ridge down through the rolling, red-clay country now called the Piedmont, and on to the coastal plain and the sea islands.

As the country differed, so did tribal laws, languages, and ways of hunting, of building, of dress.

The fierce, intelligent, and warlike Cherokees, of Iroquoian stock, were living in and near the Blue Ridge Mountains when de Soto met them on his westward march in 1540. No tribe would play a more important part in the history of the Carolinas, Georgia, and Tennessee than would these Cherokees, who claimed about forty thousand square miles of hunting grounds in the region. Their warriors wore the buckskin leggings and hunting shirts that white frontiersmen would copy later. The Cherokees were handsome people and proud of it. When smallpox, unknown before the white men's coming, scarred the Indians' faces, many committed suicide rather than live disfigured.

The Cherokees were often at war with the neighboring Catawbas, who lived in northeastern Carolina, from the Catawba River to the sea. A smaller tribe than the Cherokees, they could muster about fifteen hundred warriors when the white men arrived. By the mid-1700s, however, smallpox had wiped out all but four hundred of the tribe. The Catawbas, however, managed to stay together in spite of the white man's diseases, liquor and wars. About five hundred Catawbas live today on a reservation in York County, their old lands, just below the North Carolina line.

Along the coasts of South Carolina and Georgia lived nine tribes whose story is linked to that of the first English settlers. These Indians were cousins of the Choctaws, Creeks, and Seminoles. They included the fierce Yamassees, who would first be enemies of the Spaniards, then their friends, and wage bloody battle with the English. Other tribes were the Combahees, Ashepoos, Edistos, Stonos, Kiawahs, Cussoes, and Wandoes. Many of these Indians lived among the sea islands and were divided from each other by great stretches of swamp, wide rivers, or stretches of sea. If they had been big, warlike tribes, bent on attacking the white men, they could have wiped out the first English settlement in a few days. Instead, these tribes were among the friendliest encountered by the first explorers. They were always in fear of the tribes along the lower Savannah River, of whom the Westoes, said to be cannibals, were the fiercest.

Giovanni de Verrazano, an Italian captain sent out by France, cruised along the Atlantic coast from the Carolinas to New York, in 1524. His description of the Carolina Indians was translated into English by Richard Hakluyt, a noted geographer and friend of Sir Walter Raleigh. Hakluyt never saw the New World, but he gathered and published what French and Spanish explorers had written about it, so that future English colonists would have the information.

In Hakluyt's sixteenth-century English, Verrazano found the Indians "gentle and courteous in their manners, of sweet and pleasant countenance and comely to behold."

Their houses, he added, were made of logs and brushwood or, in summer, were sheds thatched with palm leaves and walled with woven mats that kept out the rain. While the Indians had no metal tools, Verrazano found them excellent boat builders. He wrote:

> We saw many of their boats made of one tree, twenty foote long and four foote broad, which are not made with iron or stone, or any other kind of metall (because in all this country, for the space of two hundred leagues which we ranne, we never saw one stone of any sort.) They help themselves with fire, burning so much of the tree as is sufficient for the hollowness of the boat; the like they doe in making the stern and fore part, until it be fit to sail upon the sea.

Such dug-out canoes, usually made of pine or cypress logs, were called periaguers—sometimes pettiaugers—by the early settlers. For the next 200 years they became the river transportation of the province.

The Indian towns were walled with wooden palisades. Streets, regularly laid out, often with stakes driven at the sides, led to the big "Chief's House" in the center of the settlement. Each family had a private garden patch, but all the women worked together in the tribe's corn fields. They grew pumpkins, squash, melons, beans, potatoes, and occasionally tobacco. There were peach trees and wild figs, as well as many kinds of berries that could be dried for winter rations. Hickory nuts were pressed for oil as well as eaten for food. All through the summer, smoky fires smoldered under wooden grills on which winter meat was smoked.

The Indians had no cattle, sheep, or hogs. Peter Martyr wrote that the women tamed female deer, which ran in droves through the land and penned them up, milking them like cows before letting them out in the morning. Wild ducks and geese were tamed and doubtless their eggs were eaten. Turkeys weighing as much as fifty pounds were said to roam the woods, though today a twenty-five-pound turkey is considered very large. These were shot or snared.

Seldom did Indians kill for sport. They took only the animals they needed for food or skins. To them, deer were the most useful, for their hides made clothing, their meat was food, their antlers could make any tool or weapon that must be sharp and hard. Their sinews were twisted into bowstrings or used as thread for sewing hunting shirts and moccasins. Even their brains and livers, cooked to a mush and spread over fresh hides, acted as tanning agents.

The Indians speared or trapped fish in rivers and streams inland as well as near the coast, and dried them for winter or ate them on the spot.

The largest animal hunted by the Indians of Carolina was the buffalo. The great natural grazing grounds of western Carolina swarmed with the great, shaggy beasts, called by the Cherokees *yanasa*—"the bull of God." There were elk in the same region. When the Indians hunted them, it

An engraving of a deer hunt

was with spears or arrows tipped with flint, shot from bows that the Spanish discoverers had tried in vain to draw. When white settlers moved into Carolina from Virginia and Pennsylvania, in the early 1700s, their guns soon wiped out so many of the great animals that the remaining ones fled westward where they are today.

Bears were hunted all over Carolina, from the coastal swamps to the mountains. Their skins were used as blankets. Cherokee women wove a thick, stiff cloth from the hair. They made a fragrant hair oil of bear's fat mixed with herbs.

The hardest workers were always the women. It was they who ground the corn they had planted, hoed, gathered, shucked, and shelled, in stone mortars which, among coastal tribes, had come by trade from the interior of the country. It was they who tanned deerskins so beautifully that they were almost white. Often the leather was painted in colored designs, with brews of barks and roots, and juices of berries. When the weather was too hot for deerskin clothing, the women wore little except aprons of Spanish moss or a light cloth woven from nettles prepared and spun like flax. The Spaniards found such clothing among the Chicora Indians near the coast.

Feather cloaks and hangings for chiefs' houses were also made of bird feathers arranged in patterns of brilliant colors and fastened to cloth with gum or thread.

Usually, it was the women who wove baskets and made pottery which was traded with the white settlers until the early nineteenth century. Some Carolina housewives would make no soup in iron pots when they could use Indian clay vessels. As late as the 1800s, whole families of Indians came to Charles Town with pots and baskets, selling the labor of many days for a few beads, a piece of red cloth, scissors or a knife, or a drink of the white man's rum.

Before the white men's diseases and liquor took their toll, the Carolina Indians were seldom sick.

"The Natives are very Healthfull," wrote William Hilton, an English explorer, in 1664. "We saw very many Aged among them." No wonder. The clean water they drank, the clean air they breathed, the fact that they ate vegetables when Europeans of the time ate almost none, their hard, outdoor life and scanty clothing must certainly have lengthened their lives. In case of accident or illness, however, they were not without remedies.

To sick Frenchmen and Spaniards, shaking and burning with what they called "fever and ague" but was actually malaria, the Carolina Indians gave a tea brewed from the bark of the roots of a shrub that grows widely in the deep South. The Indians called this plant "pauame." Frenchmen called it "sassafras." The spicy, mildly tonic tea made the men feel so much better that they thought they were cured.

Europeans soon came to believe that sassafras was a kind of wonder drug.

So began the great sassafras trade with the Carolina Indians, which lasted into the 1750s and formed an important export of the province. The drug was in such great demand in Europe that it was peddled in the streets, mixed with medicines and food, even carried in pockets as a kind of charm against epidemics. A list of Charles Town shipping between 1747 and 1748 shows that twenty-two tons of sassafras were shipped from the port to Europe, in just one year. Sassafras alone cured nothing. But other medicines known to the Carolina Indians are on drugstore shelves all over the world, today.

We know much about these first Americans, and yet we know so little! By the time students and historians really began asking questions about them, thousands were dead and thousands more were scattered. Today, to learn their history, we must dig into their graves or their village refuse heaps and try to guess just who they were, where they came from, and how they lived.

chapter four

The Beginning of Carolina

During the early 1500s England was a small, weak country with little manufacturing. Her big export was wool. Shipped to the Continent, it was sold to buy most things that England needed and could not manufacture. She bought cloth of every kind, from sailcloth to velvet; glass, iron, leather, felt hats, paper, lace—the list is almost endless.

By the 1580s, however, England had thousands of skilled foreign workers and a class of people with money to invest in new ventures, like colonies. The country was also filled with unemployed people who needed to leave the overcrowded island for some place where they could make a living. How had all this come about?

Thousands of fine craftsmen in the Spanish Netherlands (which included modern Belgium, Luxembourg, and parts of northrn France) were also Protestants, governed by the rigidly Catholic Spanish royal family. Their rule placed Protestants under continual pressure to change their faith.

If they resisted, their lives were made almost unbearable. By the thousands, workers and their families slipped over the borders of Protestant Holland and Germany, fled to Switzerland or made their way across the Channel to Protestant England, where they could work and worship as they chose.

France's continuing civil wars and persecutions drove thousands of highly skilled Huguenot craftsmen out of the country, too. Many sought refuge in England, where their skilled hands, experience and industrial know-how transferred whole industries to the country, and from there to the New World.

England's claims to American lands were almost as good as Spain's. In 1497, King Henry VII had given a Venetian sailor, John Cabot, and his son, Sebastian, "full and free permission to sail to all parts . . . to seek out, discover and find whatsoever isles, countries and regions which before this time, have been unknown to all Christians." In 1497 and 1498, the Cabots explored the Atlantic coast from Newfoundland to some now unknown point in the Carolinas.

More English explorers followed. One was Sir Walter Raleigh, Queen Elizabeth's great captain and sea rover, who tried to found several colonies in the vast territory loosely called Virginia. In 1585, he sent a hundred settlers to Roanoke Island, off the North Carolina coast. One year in the wilderness was too much for them. They left for home in 1586. In 1587, Raleigh landed more colonists at Roanoke. Three years later, the settlement had vanished. Its fate is still a mystery. If Raleigh's Lost Colony at Roanoke failed, the Jamestown settlement of 1607 would succeed.

In 1629, King Charles I, made a grant of land to Sir Robert Heath, his attorney-general. The grant included what are now the states of South Carolina and more than half of North Carolina; Georgia; roughly half of Tennessee; all of Alabama, Mississippi, and Louisiana; most of Arkansas; two-thirds of Oklahoma; nearly all of Texas, with a slice of northern Mexico; almost all of New Mexico and Arizona and most of southern California, and was called "Carolana."

In 1642, civil war broke out in England between the Puritans, under General Oliver Cromwell, and King Charles' followers. The Puritans won. They cut off the king's head and forced thousands of his people to leave England. Among them was Sir Robert Heath, who died, old and poor, in France.

Cromwell, the Puritan general, ruled England until his death in 1658. Two years later the dead king's son, Charles II, came home from exile and began rewarding the men who had made his return possible. In 1663, he granted the lands his father had given Heath to eight men who had done much to put him on his throne. Changing the name of the future province to "Carolina," Charles enlarged the grant, adding part of Florida, to a point just south of the the present Daytona Beach. The eight men, called Lords Proprietors, receiving this huge strip of America were: The Earl of Clarendon; the Duke of Albemarle; William, Lord Craven; John, Baron Berkeley of Stratton; Sir George Carteret; Sir John Colleton; Sir William Berkeley, and Anthony Ashley Cooper, Lord Ashley, later Earl of Shaftesbury.

The Proprietors formed a partnership and agreed to share the expense of buying ships and supplies for English settlers. The settlers would pay their own fare and that of their servants. They were to raise crops and cattle, send lumber back to England, and trade with the Indians for furs. Each Proprietor put £500 into the venture.

After the defeat and death of King Charles I, many of his followers had gone to Barbados, an island in the West

Seal of the Proprietors of Carolina

Indies, which the English had claimed in 1605. Though the island produced rich crops, it was very crowded and the settlers were anxious for more living room. In August, 1663, they sent Capt. William Hilton, in his ship, *Adventure*, to explore the Carolina coast and find a site for a Barbadian colony. He published a fascinating account of this voyage, in 1664.

In 1664, a colony of Barbadians attempted a settlement in the Cape Fear River region, in North Carolina. Storms, shipwrecks, and starvation took many lives. Finally, Capt. Robert Sandford sailed southward in the only remaining ship and reached the mouth of the North Edisto River, about twenty miles southwest of the future Charles Town. With him was young Ensign Henry Brayne, who would pilot the future Charles Town settlers home. A young surgeon, Dr. Henry Woodward, was also along. More than any other settler of Carolina, Woodward would be responsible for the success of a whole colony.

Sanford's ship was met by Shadoo, chief of the Edisto Indians, who had traveled to Barbados with Captain Hilton. Shadoo helped pilot Sanford's ship to Port Royal. There, the Cassique, or chief of the Port Royal Indians asked Sanford to take his nephew back to the wonderful island, where he might learn the language and ways of the English. Sanford agreed. Dr. Woodward asked to stay with the Port Royal Indians and learn their language and customs. The young doctor's knowledge of Indian ways made it possible for Carolina's future settlers to survive their first hard months in the wilderness, earn the Indians' trust and ultimately establish the great fur trade, source of the province's early wealth.

The Carolina settlement did not really get under way until 1669, when Sir Anthony Ashley Cooper took charge of the project. He had not crossed the Atlantic, as had two other Proprietors, Sir John Colleton, who had been a planter in Barbados, and Sir William Berkeley, who had been governor of Virginia. But Cooper had, for years, been an investor in lands and projects in the New World. He had been a shareholder in the Hudson's Bay Company, engaged in trading with the Indians of Canada, and he had also been part-owner of a sugar plantation on Barbados, in 1646. He had other investments in the New World and believed in its future. Now, with the gigantic grant of a strip of America 350 miles wide and extending from the Atlantic to the Pacific, Anthony Ashley Cooper had, for the first time, enough territory and power on which to make his dreams come true.

His friend and secretary, John Locke, one of the most learned men of the time, was engaged to draw up a system of laws for the new country. By these Fundamental Constitutions of Carolina, the country was to be governed by the Lords Proprietors and their heirs, subject only to the laws of England.

This is why Carolina was always a province, though sometimes she is called a colony. Provinces are ruled directly from the mother country. Colonies have a large measure of self-government. Any measure of local self-government achieved by Carolina would be the product of struggles against the rule of men three thousand miles away who, after all, were investors seeking the best return for their money.

Colonies make their own laws, subject to those of the mother country. Provinces have laws and governors imposed upon them. Carolina had to accept any governor sent over by the Proprietors, no matter how power-hungry or bungling or inefficient he might be. Sometimes a good and able governor arrived, and his office was always marked by progress and prosperity. Ultimately, however, the rule of strangers would force the Carolinians to revolt and appeal to the king to take them under his direct control. The spirit of independence thus gained would make Carolinians among the foremost fighters in the Revolution.

Locke's laws show that he had planned a tightly ruled country in which the settlers would have some voice in the government, but not too much. Locke stated frankly that he wished to avoid "erecting a numerous democracy." The province was to be divided into counties of 480,000 acres, or 750 square miles each. Part of each county was set aside in estates for the Proprietors. Part was reserved for the only system of nobility ever to exist in North America. These provincial nobles were to be called Landgraves and Cassiques, and rank after the Proprietors in governing the province. Landgraves had 48,000 acres each; Cassiques, 24,000. There were holdings of from 3,000 to 12,000 acres which were known as baronies—but the men who would own them would not be called barons. No Carolina title could be the same as those in England—earls, dukes, or the like. Landgrave was a German title; Cassique, the Indian word for chief.

John Locke

An American nobility sounds strange—but then, Carolina really began in a palace. As far back as 1663, letters from the Proprietors relating to Carolina are headed, "The Cockpitt." This was part of the old Palace of Whitehall, in London, built over what had been a place for cock-fights in the time of Henry VIII. The Cockpitt apartments were large, splendidly decorated rooms occupied by very important people. Cromwell had lived in the Cockpitt after he became ruler of England on the death of King Charles I. In 1663, the same apartments were occupied by the Duke of Albemarle, one of the most powerful of the Proprietors. Here the company had gathered, to discuss its new grant and investments.

Locke's laws created a parliament, a council and *eight* supreme courts, for trying different kinds of cases. It set up a series of land rents that the settlers must pay the Proprietors. The Fundamental Constitutions of Carolina were too detailed and too unworkable in other ways, but Locke's provisions for religious liberty were far ahead of any existing anywhere in the Old World or the New. Here, with the strange old spelling modernized, is Article 87 of the Fundamental Constitutions, providing for freedom of worship:

> But since the natives of that place who will be concerned in our plantations are utterly strangers to Christianity, whose idolatry, ignorance or mistake gives us no right to expel them or use them ill; and those who remove from other parts to plant there, will unavoidably be of different opinions concerning matters of religion, the liberty whereof they will expect to have allowed them, and it will not be reasonable for us on this account to keep them out; that civil peace may be maintained amidst the diversity of opinions, and our agreement and compact with all men may be duly and faithfully observed, the violation whereof, upon any pretence soever, cannot be without offense to Almighty God. . . therefore, any seven or more persons agreeing to any religion shall constitute a church or profession to which they shall give some name to distinguish it from others. . . .

"Religion, the liberty whereof they will expect to have allowed them . . ." In the whole western world, people were being driven from their homes, imprisoned, whipped, or even executed if their faith was different from that of the majority. When the first governor of Carolina read Locke's laws to the assembled settlers at Port Royal, they must have wondered if they could believe their own ears.

The Fundamental Constitutions permitted no noisy arguments over religion. Article 97 reads:

> No person shall use any reproachful, reviling or abusive language against the religion of any church or profession, it being the certain way of disturbing the public peace. . . .

Article 100 went even further:

No person whatsoever shall disturb, molest or persecute another for his speculative opinion in religion or his way of worship.

True, no free man could vote or own land in Carolina who "doth not acknowledge a God and that God is publicly and solemnly to be worshipped." Thus, Jews were free to live in Carolina, and came early to the province. So did others, persecuted elsewhere—Lutherans, Quakers, Baptists, and Huguenots.

The rights of the Indians were carefully protected, "we hoping to draw the Indians into our government," Locke had written. Later laws forbade settlers to take up lands within two and a half miles of any Indian town, if it was on the same side of a river as the settlement. Unfortunately, the Indians' rights were soon forgotten; by the first years of the eighteenth century, there would be Indian slaves in Carolina—as elsewhere in the Colonies.

In order to attract future settlers, the Proprietors offered them larger tracts of land than they could ever have possessed in England. To every free man entering the province before March 25, 1670, one hundred and fifty acres were offered, with the same amount for every black or white manservant he brought with him, and one hundred acres for every woman servant and every boy. Later, these figures were reduced. Servants were people whose ship fare was paid by a master, for whom the servant must work a certain number of years until the debt was paid in labor. Servants who had thus worked out their time would receive one hundred acres for themselves. Often, these servants were kinfolks of the masters.

The Proprietors approved Locke's Fundamental Constitutions in July, 1669, and began fitting out an expedition

for Carolina. Detailed lists were kept of the stores pur-
chased and loaded aboard the three ships which were
shortly to sail. The list reads like a small edition of a modern mail-order catalogue.

Spare sails and rigging for the ships. Food for the voyage
and for several months thereafter—biscuits, or hardtack,
flour, beef (salted, in casks), fish, cheese, oil, butter, oat-
meal, beer, brandy, peas (dried). Garden seeds, candles,
brass pots and kettles, wooden bowls and trenchers (plates);
full sets of carpenters' and blacksmiths' tools; hoes, spades,
saws, hammers, and nails; fishing nets, lines and hooks.
Clothing for the crew—red caps, shirts, and "drawers"
(pants), shoes, hammocks, beds, ruggs (blankets) and pil-
lows. Ammunition, powder, shot, a medicine chest. A thousand brick and 200 boards. A flag for the fort in Carolina
and a drum. Two hundred and forty pounds of beads for
the Indian trade, 300 hatchets, "2 gross of sizzard" (288
pairs of scissors); "10 striped suits" for chiefs' presents.
Aboard the ships were twelve guns loaned by King Charles
II "for the defense of the plantation called Carolina in the
West Indies, four iron demi-culverins and eight sacres. . . ."
These were long-range guns, taking shots of twelve pounds
and six pounds. Today they would look like toys.

Late in August, 1669, the Carolina expedition sailed
from Gravesend, part of the port of London. They passed
through the mouth of the Thames River, and headed westward through the Straits of Dover into the English Channel. The frigate *Carolina*, the flagship, was a 200-ton vessel,
slightly larger than the *Mayflower*. She was accompanied
by the frigate *Port Royal*, 100 tons, and the shallop *Albemarle*, 30 tons, a small, light craft suitable for sailing up
shallow streams.

In command was young Joseph West, whom the Proprietors seem to have trusted completely. The passenger
list of the *Carolina* shows 93 names, but, from the settlers'

letters, we know this list was incomplete. The *Port Royal* and *Albemarle* were crowded, too. In all, about 148 men, women, and children sailed aboard the three vessels.

On the Proprietors' orders, they stopped at Kinsale, in southern Ireland, where it was hoped some Irish "servants" would join the party. None did, and several passengers left the ships. Then the expedition headed south-southwest for Barbados, where other settlers would come aboard. There, Sir John Yeamans would replace West as commander of the expedition, and name a governor—who might be himself.

We know West's orders from the detailed letters the Proprietors wrote. The settlers must first build good, tight houses and storehouses, then start raising money crops as soon as possible. Nobody knew what would grow in Carolina, so West was to get seed and roots from Thomas Colleton, son of the Proprietor, Sir John, and a planter on Barbados.

"You are to furnish y'selfe with Cotton Seed, Ginger Roots, wch roots you are to carry planted in a tubb of earth, y^t they may not dye before yor arrival att Port Royall; alsoe you may in another tubb carry some Canes planted for a tryall—alsoe of ye severall sorts of vines of that Island & some Ollive setts. . . ." If any of these crops succeeded, the Proprietors' investment would soon be profitable. Young Colleton was also to furnish the expedition with six young sows and a boar. Cattle were to be bought in Virginia after the settlement was established.

The little fleet came safely to Barbados. On October 2, 1669, as the ships lay at anchor, a wild hurricane swept over the West Indies. When it passed, the *Albemarle* lay wrecked on the harbor rocks. The *Port Royal* and *Carolina* were badly damaged. It was mid-November before the ships sailed again with a borrowed shallop, the *Three Brothers*, replacing the wrecked *Albemarle*. During the voyage and the time lost for repairs, much of the ships'

Yeamans' little fleet

food had been eaten. Still, Carolina was only a short sail away.

At the last minute, Sir John Yeamans found he could not go to Carolina. He appointed as governor seventy-nine-year-old Col. William Sayle, of Bermuda. "A man of no great sufficiency," wrote Yeamans gloomily, "yet the best I could get."

Joseph West, leader of the expedition, was a commoner, a man without rank, hence he could not be named as governor. Sayle, despite his age, was preferred because he was a gentleman of good family, though not of the nobility. A Puritan, Sayle had twice been governor of Bermuda and was used to ruling men.

He could have refused the appointment which would take him away from his wife and comfortable home into a wilderness full of dangers and hardships. Instead, Sayle accepted the governorship of Carolina and, with a few Negro slaves and his son, Nathaniel, sailed for the land where he must have known he would end his days. A long-past disappointment probably influenced his decision.

In 1648, William Sayle had tried to found his own colony, based on absolute freedom of worship. In fact, one was not required to worship any God at all.

Parliament granted him the island of Eleuthera, in the Bahamas. His ship was wrecked almost at the end of the voyage, but even before that, a troublemaker had set the colonists quarrelling among themselves.

For months, sixty-nine marooned settlers barely existed on the wild birds and fish they caught. Finally, Sayle and eight men took the ship's tender and went for help, not knowing where winds and currents might take them. The Gulf Stream swept them northward to the mouth of the Nancimond River, in Virginia, where Puritan colonists rescued Sayle and his men, giving them a larger boat and plentiful food.

These Virginia Puritans were considering moving from their settlement. Sayle begged them to join his colony on Eleuthera. The Virginians were seriously considering this plan when Sayle showed them his charter, granting absolute freedom of conscience. The Virginians changed their minds.

Freedom to worship as Puritans was one thing; freedom to worship any way at all—or no way—was too much. Sadly, Sayle returned to Eleuthera, rescued his settlers, and saw them scatter. His colony, founded on the great ideal of religious liberty, had failed.

Now, near his life's end, William Sayle saw one last chance to help another colony, devoted to religious freedom, succeed. To see the dream of his life come true, though he paid for it with death in the wilderness must have made him answer, "Yes!" to Yeamans' question, "Will you go?"

chapter five

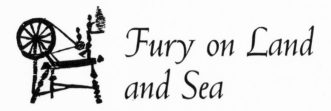 *Fury on Land and Sea*

In late November, 1669, the three ships sailed for Carolina again. In early December, they touched the island of Nevis, in the West Indies and there found Dr. Henry Woodward who had been left behind in Carolina. Raiding Spaniards had captured him and taken him to St. Augustine. There, an English buccaneer, Capt. Robert Searle, had raided the town and set the English prisoners free. Woodward had joined Searle's ship as surgeon. The same hurricane that had wrecked the *Albemarle* at Barbados had sunk Searle's ship off Nevis, where Woodward had come ashore. He joined the Carolina expedition.

At Bermuda, the ships took on Sayle and his party. Scarcely had they left Bermuda than another hurricane swooped down upon them.

The ships lost sight of each other. The pilot who had come aboard the *Port Royal* at Bermuda soon confessed he was lost. For six long weeks, the frigate, with forty-four passengers, blundered through the Caribbean, until her water gave out. Turning back towards Bermuda, she struck a coral reef near the island of Abaco and was wrecked on January 12, 1670.

The passengers were saved. The ship's carpenter, however, went mad and refused to build a boat from the wreckage, that might take the survivors to safety. He grew so violent that the captain marooned him on another island. Captain Russell and the passengers patched together a small boat from the timbers of the *Port Royal* and reached Eleuthera where they hired a shallop that took them back to Bermuda. There, they found the battered *Carolina*, which had also turned back. Her stern was smashed, half her guns gone, her supplies lost or spoiled. Nobody knew what had happened to the *Three Brothers*. She had simply vanished in the storm.

With Captain Henry Brayne at her helm, the *Carolina* and a borrowed sloop with the *Port Royal*'s passengers again sailed for Port Royal. They strayed past the intended landing place and first sighted the Carolina coast at Seewee (Bulls) Bay, some twenty miles northeast of the future Charles Town.

Going ashore, the settlers were greeted by Indians shouting "Bony conraro Angles!"—bad Spanish for "Good English comrade!" Here, too, was the Cassique, or Chief, of Kiawah, the country around the future Ashley River. The Cassique had traded with the Cape Fear Barbadian colony, had sailed with Robert Sandford, and was a firm friend of the English. He came aboard the *Carolina* and guided the settlers to Port Royal harbor, their intended landing place. They found the Port Royal Indians in a panic, for the savage, man-eating Westoes had just raided the surrounding country. They pleaded with the Englishmen to settle among them and protect them with their guns.

The Cassique of Kiawah disagreed. He showed the English how dangerously near the Spaniards their Port Royal settlement would be. He pleaded with the Englishmen to settle in his own country where two wide rivers, with a long peninsula between them, emptied into a fine harbor. Everything was better in the Kiawah country, said the Cassique. Governor Sayle sent a few men in a small boat to explore.

Returning, they agreed with the Cassique. The settlers, exhausted, their clothing shabby and salt-stiffened, hungry for land under their feet, argued hotly whether to stay or go, but in the end, the Cassique had his way.

Early in April, 1670, the ships dropped anchor in the Ashley River, at a spot just across from the present Citadel, the military college of South Carolina.

They settled on a low bluff, the first land on the north side of a winding creek—Old Town Creek, they call it now. The point of land, overgrown with pines, ran out into the wide Ashley River marshes. A few miles up this river that Robert Sandford had named for the Proprietor who had really made this expedition possible, the settlement was well hidden from the guns of Spain's Silver Fleet. On one side, the steep banks of the creek protected the site. On the river side, the marsh was flooded at high tide and was a sea of deep, slippery mud when the tide was out. The narrow neck of land behind the settlement was guarded by a ditch and palisade.

Six weeks after the landing, a battered little sloop, the *Three Brothers*, lost in the hurricane that had wrecked the *Port Royal*, sailed into Ashley River. Twelve of her passengers were missing. The storm had whirled her north as far as the mouth of the Nancimond River, in Virginia. After repairs, she had turned south, missed Port Royal, and blundered into Spanish country at Guale, now St. Catherine's Island, off the Georgia coast. There, ten men had gone ashore to hunt fresh meat, and two women with bundles of washing had accompanied them. The Indians had captured them all, killed eight, and turned over the

Settlers in South Carolina

rest to the Spaniards. After vainly trying to get her people back, the *Three Brothers* had to go on without them. Sailing up the coast, the little craft saw canoes approaching. The Indians hailed them and, through Shadoo, a native who had been at Barbados with Captain William Hilton, told them "there were English at Kiawah." The next day, he guided them to the mouth of the Ashley, up its wide stream—and home.

About one hundred twenty settlers at home at last, after a nine-month horror of a voyage that none of them would ever forget! They were a government, too, for, at Port Royal, Governor Sayle had held an election, as directed by the Lords Proprietors. Even they had realized that Locke's laws were made for the future of the province when it would be home to thousands of people. Five Council members had been elected by the settlers, to serve with five others, acting for the Lords Proprietors.

Food was already short. The *Three Brothers* was sent to Bermuda for supplies; the *Carolina* to Virginia to buy hogs and the little black cattle which multiplied amazingly, though the settlers wrote home that the beasts were under-sized and overpriced. With both ships away, Henry Wood-ward traded with the Indians for food to keep the settlement going until the ships returned. He also explored the country far inland, making friends with the Indians and laying the foundations for Carolina's rich fur trade that would last for more than a century.

Woodward had just returned from a journey when the friendly Indians nearer the sea sent word that three Spanish ships lay off shore. They also said that thirty canoes filled with Spaniards and Indians were waiting at the mouth of the Stono River, a few miles south of Albemarle Point, where the settlement was located. The enemy must have thought that with both ships away, the settlers would be hungry and their defenses weak. The Spaniards would at-tack the *Carolina,* if she returned, and sink her before she could land supplies. Meanwhile, the Indians would attack Albemarle Point, itself.

Grimly, the settlers hurried to their small fort and trained the cannon from the *Carolina* on the attackers. The Indians had not expected such big guns, and they fled. Just then, the *Carolina* sailed in past the Spaniards who turned and made for St. Augustine, without firing a shot.

Now they had enough food for eight months. The first threat of attack was past. It was August 23, 1670.

"Wee are here setled in the very chaps of the Spaniard!" wrote Joseph Dalton, a Council member, to Lord Ashley.

"God will preserve me as He hath in many Dangers when I saw His wonders in ye Deepe and was by Him delivered," wrote Mrs. Affra Coming, wife of the *Carolina*'s first mate.

Tired though the settlers were, they still took time to send the first products of Carolina to the Proprietors, via Bermuda. The next ship leaving Carolina carried twelve cedar "planks"—red, fragrant logs, squared neatly by Eng-lish axes.

chapter six

Carolina Grows

Slowly the province grew. More Barbadians came. The land near the settlement at Albemarle Point and up the river was parcelled out in large grants—the beginnings of future great plantations. The people were discovering what grew best in Carolina. The first winter, an ice storm killed the oranges, the lime trees brought from Barbados, as well as the ginger plants. The olive trees would grow and bear, but later freezes would kill them. It was soon discovered, however, that cotton, tobacco, and indigo would make good crops. A barrel of seed rice sent by the Proprietors and scattered in low, muddy spots grew very well.

There was little or no money in the province. Farm produce, deerskins and lumber were used instead for barter. A ship's fare to Carolina from Barbados was paid with 500 to 1,000 pounds of sugar. Henry Woodward's ever widening Indian trade brought beautifully tanned deerskins and furs for trade with England. The hogs from Virginia multiplied as they were turned loose in the woods to fatten on "mast"—

Persons Names to whom granted	Number of Acres	In what County Parish or Township or on what River or Creek Situated	Date of the Grant	In What rent reserved thereon if any
Lady Margaret Yamans	1070	on Yaman's Creek	9th Feb.y 1674	
Anthony Earl of Shaftsbury	12000	on Ashley River	18th March 1675	
Joseph Pendarvis	137		1st Jan.y 1675	
Mathew English &c } John Morgan }	140	on Wando River		
John Smyth	1300	on Ashley River	25th Novem.r 1675	
Stephen Bull	400	on Do.	28th October 1676	
William Jones	210	on Stevan's Island	10th Jan.y 1676	
Maurice Mathews	402	on Ashley River	28th April 1676	
John Boone	200		20th Feb.y 1676	
S.r Peter Colleton Kn.t } & Tho.s Colleton Esq.r }	373	near Do.	20th Sep.r 1677	—
Edward Mathews	570	on Cooper River	15th April 1676	
Robert Donne	150	near Charles Town	5th August 1676	

A list of land grants in South Carolina from 1674–76

literally millions of live-oak acorns that peppered the ground in autumn. Soon, Carolina hams and bacon were being shipped even to New England.

Cattle grew well. Men who had arrived as "servants" were now farming acres of their own, and possessed as many as 500 or 1,000 cattle. The settlers began to breed horses. The rich land produced fine crops of corn, peas, and potatoes.

Soon, ships were being routed so that none ever travelled empty and each voyage made a profit. One of Capt. Henry Brayne's letters to the Proprietors shows how he planned to load the *Carolina* with lumber (which cost nothing), to be traded in Barbados for sugar and rum. This cargo would go to New York, and be traded for cattle and provisions. More settlers might return with the ship, perhaps paying their fare with gold or silver coins.

Old Governor Sayle, worn out with age and hardships, was very ill. A few hours before he died on March 4, 1671, he gathered the Council about him and appointed Joseph

West as the new governor. The people were very glad of this, for they all liked and trusted West, who had commanded the ships all through their terrible voyage.

During the governor's last months of life, people had written complaining letters to England, about the old governor's continued illness. Some even suggested that he was losing his mind. None could deny, however, that William Sayle showed very good sense on two occasions.

It was he who had selected the site of the future Charles Town, a place easily defended and which, with its great harbor, must become a fine port for the province's trade. And he had appointed as his successor Joseph West, possibly the most able of Carolina's early governors.

In 1680, it was decided to move the settlement to the peninsula, its present site. The Albemarle Point cabins were abandoned to decay. Today, however, the settlement is being excavated, and many interesting things have been discovered—pottery, glass, long-stemmed clay pipes, old bricks.

As early as 1671, the new Charles Town, so named by the Proprietors' orders, had been planned and platted like a modern subdivision. A "Grand Modell" of the town was sent over, divided in 335 lots and very broad streets laid out at right angles to each other, like those of a Roman town. John Oldmixon, a British historian who wrote *A History of the British Empire in North America* in 1708, commented:

> . . . a model of a town was sent, which it will be well, if the people of Carolina are able to build 100 years hence; but the Proprietors, as appears by their constitutions and instructions to their Governours, thought 'twas as easy to build towns as to draw schemes.

Though the settlers followed the general plan of the Grand Modell, they could not make it fit the peninsula, which was laced with ponds, tidal creeks, and marshes. Like many a Dutch city, much of Charles Town was reclaimed from the waters.

By the end of 1680, there were thirty houses in the town, with more going up all the time. Thomas Ashe, clerk of the ship *Richmond*, which arrived from England in 1680, wrote of young Charles Town:

> It's very commodiously scituated from many other Navigable Rivers that lie near it on which the Planters are seated; by the advantage of Creeks, which have a communication from one great River to another, at the Tide or Ebb the Planters may bring their Commodities to the Town to the Common Market and Magazine both for Trade and Shipping. The Town is regularly laid out into large and capacious Streets, which to buildings is a great Ornament and Beauty. In it they have reserved convenient places for building of a Church, Town-House and other Publick Structures, an Artillery Ground for the Exercise of their Militia, and Wharfs for the Convenience of their Trade and Shipping. At our being there [1680] was judged in the Country 1000 or 1200 souls; but the great Numbers of Families from England, Ireland, Barbadoes, Jamaica and the Caribees [Caribbean Islands] which daily Transport themselves thither, have more than doubled that number. . . .

For many years, creeks and rivers were the chief roads of Carolina, and Carolina was a one-city province. All land and water routes led to Charles Town. From plantations along the Ashley and Cooper rivers, the Wando, Stono, and Edisto, came boats bringing families down to the capital for shopping or to attend church. Boats and barges piled high with rice would be poled from plantation landings on creeks to the rivers and floated down to Charles Town's waiting ships. Bales of skins, barrels of pitch and turpentine, piles of lumber lay ready on the wharves. As the wealth of the province grew, so did her hopes.

chapter seven

New People
and Hard Times

For more than a century, the Huguenots—French Protestants—had been persecuted for their faith. They were among France's best farmers and finest craftsmen. Now they were coming to the New World. On April 20, 1680, when the new Charles Town was a small group of cabins on the banks of the Cooper River, the ship *Richmond,* from England, brought forty-five Huguenots to Carolina.

These people had been refugees in England, waiting and hoping to get passage to the New World. After long delays, King Charles II had loaned the *Richmond,* loading cargo for Barbados, to a group of Huguenots. Since many refugees arrived with little money and less baggage, the king loaned the expedition £1,500. In return, the Huguenots promised to raise silk worms and to manufacture in Carolina the beautiful velvets, damasks, and satins that only France, the Low Countries, and Italy had produced. They promised to plant vineyards and make wine which England would no longer have to buy from France, her old enemy. They would plant olive trees and produce fine oil. When the Richmond sailed from England on December 17, 1679, she carried the roots of fine French grapevines and some wooden frames on which lay twigs dotted with pale blue specks—silkworm eggs. They were not supposed to hatch until spring.

As the ship moved into warm, southern seas, however, the silkworms hatched too soon. There were no piles of fresh mulberry leaves for them to feed on, so they starved to death. Sadly, the Huguenots threw them overboard. Again, they seemed to be landing in a strange country, empty-handed.

The *Richmond*'s passenger list is lost, so we know the names of only a few of these refugees. We do know, however, that no sooner did these people come ashore than they began making themselves useful. As in England, they set up looms and spinning wheels and began making cloth of Carolina flax and wool. Others made good bricks of the local clay—a new industry for the province. Still others spread through the wilderness around Charles Town, draining swamps, taming the land, particularly around the Santee River, some forty miles northwest of Charles Town. This district was so filled with refugees that it was long known as "French Santee."

In Charles Town, they opened schools or took special pupils in music, dancing, drawing, needlework, and mathematics. Often they taught Latin, Greek, and fencing—swordplay—very necessary in a time when many men went armed.

Huguenot merchants in Charles Town were so hardworking and trustworthy that their business prospered from the beginning. "As honest as a Huguenot," and "as rich as a Huguenot" became bywords in Charles Town as they had been in France.

Huguenot planters, having tamed the wilderness mostly

by their own labor, for at first they owned few slaves, soon found that rice and indigo, almost the only blue dye used in the western world, brought more money than the silk and grapevines they had come to raise. Soon, also, the refugees were improving farming methods and even inventing farm machines.

In 1691, a Huguenot watchmaker, Pierre Jacob Guérard, son of the organizer of the *Richmond* expedition, got a patent from the Assembly for a "pendulum engine" which removed the tough husks from the rice grains. Until that time, rice had been thrashed by pounding a few handfuls at a time with heavy, clublike pestles in a log hollowed out at one end. This old process never died out, but Guérard's machine marked the beginning of mechanical farm tools in Carolina. The sons and grandsons of other émigrés would devise rice mills which handled still larger crops.

From these people who came to Carolina with little but their skills, their character and their faith, came such builders of America as Francis Marion, the "Swamp Fox" of the Revolution; Henry Laurens, president of the Continental Congress, 1777–78; Gabriel Manigault, who loaned the state $220,000 at the beginning of the Revolution, fought to defend the city when he was seventy-six years old, and was imprisoned for his patriotism.

Many groups of emigrants came to Charles Town, over the years, but it was the Huguenots, above all, who transformed the province and contributed to every phase of its development.

By the end of the seventeenth century, the white population of Charles Town had grown to five thousand very busy people. The harbor was crowded with ships from Europe, the West Indies, and the northern colonies. They were loaded with barrels of tar, pitch, and turpentine, called naval stores, because they were used to keep ships tight and seaworthy. On wharves, in warehouses were bales of furs and barrels of deerskins for shipment to Europe. Already there were barrels of Carolina rice, too, and piles of lumber and bundles of pipe-staves—oak slats from which barrels were made. Ships from New York and Boston took away barrels of salt beef for winter food and for long voyages.

Every ship from the Indies brought sugar, rum, and often slaves. English ships arrived with everything not yet manufactured in the province—shoes, hats, swords, and guns; sheet lead for molding bullets; powder, drugs, glass, paper, pins, needles, saws, axes, books, paint—the list is almost endless.

Down Indian paths and through waterways leading to Charles Town came food from the surrounding farms and plantations—fruits, vegetables, beef, pork, chicken, rice, corn, and beans. For trade goods equal to about twenty-five dollars a year, a plantation owner could hire an Indian hunter who would keep his family supplied with all the fish and game it could use.

Into this busy, hopeful place came the first of several tragedies, beginning in midsummer, 1697. In a letter dated March 12, 1698, the governor and Council wrote the news to the Proprietors:

> We have had the Small pox amongst us nine or ten months, which hath been very infectious and mortal. We have lost by the distemper [disease] 200 or 300 persons. And on the 24 February a fire broke out in the night in Charles Town which hath burnt the dwellings, stores and out-houses of at least fifty families and hath consumed (it is generally believed) in houses and goods the value of £30,000 sterling.

While the city was still burying its dead, an earthquake shook the land, killing nobody but frightening the sick and discouraged population into wondering whether they had better not move to some safer place. Worse still, an epidemic among the cattle killed them by the thousands.

Hunger threatened the province while clouds of buzzards wheeled overhead.

Then, some ship from the West Indies brought in a new form of death—yellow fever. On January 17, 1699, a letter to the Proprietors from the Council reported that the fever had killed 150 people between August and November. Public officials, the minister and several judges had died. Another letter, reporting 160 more deaths, added that "the Town is thinned to a very few people."

In the autumn of 1699, a hurricane struck the coast, dashing waves over the town walls, driving people to the top stories of their houses. None died on land. Only the ship *Rising Sun,* already crippled by storms and limping into port with the survivors of an unsuccessful Scottish colony from Panama, was dashed to pieces. All aboard her perished. The only survivors were the Reverend Archibald Stobo, who had been invited to preach in Charles Town that day, his wife, and some of the ship's officers. They owed their lives to a sermon!

Six disasters in three years! But Charles Town kept growing. One reason was her magnificent harbor. Her Indian trade was another reason for her wealth. But Carolina owed much of her progress to her laws guaranteeing religious liberty.

By 1675, Quakers, unwelcome in England and the northern colonies, were flocking to Carolina with the help of the Earl of Shaftesbury, formerly Lord Ashley. In that year, he wrote to Andrew Percival, his agent in the province:

> There come now in my Dogger [a two-masted fishing boat] Jacob Waite and two or three other familys of those who are called Quakers. These are but the Harbingers of a greater Number to follow. . . . I would have you be very kind to them and give them all the assistance you can. . . . For they are a people I have a great Regard to. . . .

Charles Town harbor in 1739

The province was a melting pot of faiths. So many Huguenots poured in that the Proprietors had special tracts of land set aside for them. In 1696, a congregation of Baptists, expelled from Maine (then part of Massachusetts Bay Colony) moved, with their minister, Mr. William Screven, to Carolina. Settling first on the Cooper River, they moved later into Charles Town. There, William Elliott gave them a lot on Church Street. The First Baptist Church of Charleston is still on that spot.

Scottish Presbyterians from Stuart's Town, a colony planted near Port Royal in 1684 and soon wiped out by Spaniards and Indians, were already in the province. In 1695, a group of missionary Puritans from Dorchester, Massachusetts, moved to Carolina, where they founded the town of Dorchester near what is now Summerville. Finding the climate unhealthy, they moved on to Georgia, leaving a few tabby walls and some old graves as their memorial. By 1697, a few Jews, persecuted elsewhere, had arrived. Mean-

while, well-to-do Barbadian planters, all Church of England people, were coming in increasing numbers with slaves to work their new plantations.

There would not always be peace in such a mixture of religious and political opinions. Puritans would resent the Church of England's prayer book and forms of worship. The English would object to Huguenot ways and their swift political prominence. Hot words would fly; there would be brawls in the streets and the Council. But nobody was whipped, hanged, imprisoned, or expelled from Carolina for his faith.

In 1704, a surveyor, Edward Crisp, drew a map of Charles Town that showed buildings as well as streets. There, within a few blocks of each other, one sees the English Church, the Independent (Congregational), Anabaptist (Baptist) and French churches, and the Quaker Meeting House. In the seventeenth century, there were few places on earth where such a map could have been drawn.

chapter eight

The Walled City
Meets Her Foes

In 1702, France and Spain were at war with England on both sides of the world. As usual, everything happening in Europe directly affected the American colonies. This time, Carolina was particularly threatened.

France was bent on establishing a great empire stretching from Canada down the Mississippi valley to the Gulf of Mexico, where Louisiana had been settled in 1682. Here, the French ran into Carolina's sphere of influence. Her great fur trade stretched from Charles Town to the Mississippi, a distance of about a thousand miles. Neither the Carolina traders nor the Lords Proprietors had any intention of giving up the trade that was bringing in far more money than any crops grown in the province.

Spain, too, was angry that the English had managed to remain on territory she still regarded as part of Florida. As the war dragged on, France and Spain decided to wipe out Carolina. Since Charles Town was, in effect, the province

—apart from a few outlying settlements and traders' routes— the enemies of Carolina were sure that once Charles Town fell, the whole province would be at their mercy.

Learning what the French and Spaniards intended, Carolina struck first.

In 1702, Governor James Moore and Col. Robert Daniell headed a force of five hundred settlers and a large number of Indians in an attack on St. Augustine. They found the town empty, for the population had retreated into Fort San Marcos, which was well stocked with food and ammunition, and had sent to Havana for help. Moore's little cannons might have been BB guns, for all their effect on the fort's stout walls of coquina rock and "tabby"—a sand and oyster-shell concrete. Moore sent Daniell to Jamaica for bombs and heavier guns, while he continued the siege.

Before Daniell could return, two big Spanish men-of-war came sailing in while Moore, attacking by land, was helpless to save his ships. He burned them as they lay at anchor, destroying his supplies at the same time. Then he burned St. Augustine—homes, churches, warehouses. He retreated by land to Charles Town, leaving the Spaniards panic-stricken and homeless. But Moore had also saddled the province with a war debt.

To raise cash, Carolina printed her first paper money. Gold and silver were so rare that Spanish coins were used by Carolinians and the law set their value in pounds. The paper money became worth less and less until the province was in real financial trouble.

In 1703, Moore, at his own expense, mustered fifty white settlers and a thousand friendly Indians and swept south-westward into the country around what is now Tallahassee, Florida. His Indians made short work of the Apalachees living there, and Moore's troops burned five fortified Indian towns and several missions and carried away thirteen hundred Apalachees as slaves.

These English raids shook Spain's hold on the whole southeast and ended her hopes of regaining the parts of Georgia and Alabama that she claimed. More and more settlers retreated to the protection of St. Augustine. Eleven years later, English claims to Georgia and part of Alabama were almost unquestioned.

The same raids, however, alarmed the French at Mobile. Since 1702, they had been developing a plan of attack on Carolina. In August, 1705, Spain and France agreed that ships of both nations, based in Havana for the attack, should capture Charles Town at the earliest possible opportunity and drive out the English forever.

How much of this plan was actually known in London and Charles Town is uncertain. Still, Carolinians could foresee what would happen. In 1703, Governor Moore was replaced by Sir Nathaniel Johnson, a former governor of the Leeward Islands in the Caribbean. A Charles Town clerk wrote, "His presence gave great Encouragement to yᵉ people who had a great Confidence in his Conduct, he having been bredd abroad a soldier from his Youth." At the time, the governor's military record was so well known that nobody bothered to say what it was.

There was only one war in which Nathaniel Johnson could have taken part in his youth. This was the War of the Spanish Netherlands, in which England joined Holland and Sweden against France, from 1667 to 1668. Nathaniel Johnson, born in 1645, was just twenty-one in 1666 when he was absent from England for two years. He was knighted by King Charles II in 1680.

The War of the Spanish Netherlands was fought over lowlying lands, laced with creeks and marshes, very much like coastal Carolina. Many battles took place around fortified towns facing the sea, or on rivers. On his arrival in Carolina, the governor promptly began fortifying Charles Town. The design of the walls he placed around her was much like those in the Netherlands and along the French coast, designed by the great French engineer, Vauban, whose fortifications revolutionized the art of warfare in the eighteenth century.

On Windmill Point, at the entrance to Charles Town's harbor, the governor built a small triangular fort. One hundred and fifty years later, Fort Johnson would still be defending Charleston Harbor. The old soldier laid in stores, mounted his guns, drilled the militia. Now, let them come!

Then yellow fever struck Charles Town.

Again people fled into the country. Again bonfires blazed in the streets to clear the air, and physicians stood by helplessly or dosed their patients with tar water or a concoction called the "Vinegar of the Four Thieves." Men who had seemed healthy a few hours before twisted in agony on their straw mattresses, vomiting uncontrollably, their skin turning bronze-yellow before they died. Corpses were piled in wagons for burial in the common grave outside the walls.

On Saturday, August 24, 1706, the governor was at his plantation, Silk Hope, more than twenty miles up the Cooper River from Charles Town. He had left peppery Col. William Rhett in command of the town. Into Rhett's headquarters, the Watch House, built over a semicircular fortification called the Half Moon Battery, hurried a Dutch captain, Peter Stool, whose ship, the *Flying Horse*, had left Charles Town a few days before.

Stool had headed for St. Augustine, hoping to waylay and capture a Spanish ship coming in with gold to pay the garrison. Instead, he had tangled with a French ship that had nearly sunk him. The day before, four other ships had chased him. A fleet must be gathering. . . .

BOOM!

It was the signal gun on Oyster Point, at the southern tip of the peninsula. Through the Watch House windows, Stool and Rhett saw five curls of smoke rising over

Colonel William Rhett

Sullivan's Island at the harbor's mouth. Five ships sighted.

Charles Town's alarm guns sounded. Rhett sent a messenger for the governor. The French-Spanish fleet arrived outside the harbor bar that evening but dared not try to cross it in the darkness. Rhett sent riders to call his plantation militia. Would the men dare to come into the plague-stricken town, even to defend it, he wondered?

Next morning, the plantation men began arriving. The governor's son-in-law, Thomas Broughton, must have ridden all night from Mulberry, his plantation some twenty miles up the Cooper River. Three companies of militia marched bravely into town. Governor Johnson arrived with more men. Nobody seemed afraid of the fever.

Next morning, the enemy crossed the bar with a fair wind and tide. Though nothing lay between them and the town, they anchored near Sullivan's Island and stayed there. Monsieur le Feboure, commander of the fleet, had seen those walls of the latest European design, and had guessed their strength. While he hesitated, the governor ordered all the militia into town and had every house in Charles Town lighted at night for as long as the enemy were present. He knew they had learned of the fever in the town. That was why they were attacking now. Well, they should find no darkened, besieged, scared city mourning its dead. That night Charles Town's candle-lit windows glared at the foe across the black waters of the harbor.

Next day, sixty Huguenot planters, commanded by Captain Longbois arrived, having ridden night and day from the Santee River district, more than fifty miles north of Charles Town.

The six small ships in the harbor were armed, and a fire ship prepared—an old hulk loaded with powder, tar, turpentine, tallow—to be sent, all sails set, into the midst of the enemy fleet.

Le Feboure sent a messenger with a flag of truce and a demand to surrender the city within the hour. The governor had him blindfolded and taken around the fortifications. At intervals, the bandage was removed, so that he could see ranks of armed men. He never knew they were the same troops, rushed from place to place just ahead of the Frenchman and his guards. Then, wrote a Charles Town clerk to the Proprietors:

> The Governor by an Interpreter told him that it needed not a Quarter of an Hour nor a minute's time to give Answer to that demand, for that he [the messenger] could see that he [the governor] was not in a condition to be obliged to surrender the town. And that he would keep the same, and defend it, in the name and by the authority of his Mistress, the Queen of England.
>
> Whereupon the Messenger took his leave, departing to the Ships, seeming very much surprised at our Strength and Numbers.

The enemy began slipping ashore, burning plantations here and there, feasting on the cattle and hogs they shot. Led by friendly Indians, the Carolinians would surprise the

French and Spaniards while they were sleeping off the effects of the barbecue, and take prisoners before the invaders could fire a shot.

"Seeing our men running on Huzzaing" wrote the clerk, "with a desperate resolution to Engage them Closer, they Immediately Quitt the field and fled away in great Disorder and Confusion." For days, the militia were rounding up prisoners and bringing them into Charles Town.

For the first time, Carolinians had beaten off a foreign, seaborne invader, as they would do in 1776, just seventy short years away. For the first time, plantations and town had stood together to repulse a foe.

On August 31, six Carolina ships and the fire ship moved out towards Sullivan's Island, where the enemy fleet still hesitated. Aiming the fire ship straight at the French admiral's galley, the skeleton crew lashed the rudder into position, set the sails, lighted the long slow-matches which led to the powder below decks, and slipped overboard. Naturally, there was smoke. Aboard the big French ship with its white lily-flag, drums rattled, whistles shrilled. A shower of musket shot skipped harmlessly over the water. Then the wind caught the fire ship, driving her into the midst of the fleet. Anchors were almost snatched from the water and the fleet lumbered out to sea.

Next day, all seemed clear. Then word came that a big ship had been sighted in Seewee (Bull's) Bay, about twenty miles northeast of Charles Town. This was the galley of Monsieur Arbousett, the invaders' land general, with about two hundred soldiers aboard.

Peter Stool's little *Flying Horse* and a sloop with Colonel Rhett and some militia sailed for Seewee, where they found the big galley making repairs to her rigging. She struck her colors and surrendered. The total taken was close to two hundred fifty prisoners.

"And thus through the Providence of Almighty God the

The French messenger was led blindfolded around the fortifications

Malicious Designs of Oͬ Enemies are defeated and their Fleet like a Second Spanish Armada who, had she succeeded, intended nothing more than the utter ruine and destruction of the flourishing Collony," wrote the clerk. He added praise for the sixty-one-year-old governor:

> Near wore out with age and pain, he forgot nothing of the duty of a great Commandͬ, being frequently on Horseback at all hours of the night to see his Orders Executed and infusing by his Example life and courage among the people resolved not to outlive the fate of the Province.

Nathaniel Johnson's portrait, painted the year of his victory, shows him in black armor. Under a high, curly brown

Nathaniel Johnson

wig, his long face, with deep circles under the dark eyes, looks sad and stubborn. He would be removed as governor in 1709, after some highhanded dealings in the Indian trade and would end his days quietly at Silk Hope, raising silkworms.

The fact remains that this victory of Carolinians over a comparatively small foreign fleet may have changed the history of this country. A victorious Spain, entrenched in Carolina, would have commanded the land all the way to the French Mississippi. Virginia would have come under French-Spanish attack and the New England colonies would have been caught in a pincers movement between Spain, on the south, and French Canada on the north. The whole eastern coast of North America would have become a battleground for Indians, Frenchmen, Spaniards, and Englishmen, all fighting for possession of the land.

Nathaniel Johnson's courage had unified Carolina. As the militia came to Charles Town's defense, as one man's orders marched healthy country boys into a dying town and made its fate their own, the province thought and acted for the first time as a united and independent power.

chapter nine

The Yamassee Terror

Even before Charles Town's new walls and the courage of her governor and people had stopped an enemy invasion, Carolinians had realized how alone they really were. Whether the province survived or perished depended on her people alone. Little or no help could be expected from England or the other colonies.

More than three hundred miles of wilderness separated Charles Town from Williamsburg, Virginia, the nearest colonial capital. The only land travel between was by Indian paths that often vanished in vast, coastal swamps.

To reach the northern colonies by sea was just as dangerous. The reason was Cape Hatteras, a long, narrow strip of sand along the North Carolina coast. Hatteras curves far out into the Atlantic and comes very near the Gulf Stream which swings up from the Gulf of Mexico and follows the general outline of the Atlantic coast before curving northeastward towards Europe. The Gulf Stream's warm currents, meeting the cool land breezes of Hatteras produce sudden, violent storms which were particularly dangerous to sailing vessels with primitive navigation instruments. Hatteras' wreck-strewn coast was called "The Graveyard of Ships."

Because of Hatteras, it was safer and easier to sail from Charles Town to England than from Charles Town to Boston, Philadelphia, or New York. An accident of sand-bars, winds, and ocean currents divided the American colonies into a close-knit northern group, while, to the south, Carolina, a city-state, since only the country around Charles Town was settled, must be doubly independent because of her isolation.

Comparatively quick, easy communication existed between Massachusetts, New Hampshire, Rhode Island, Connecticut, New York, New Jersey, Pennsylvania, Delaware, Maryland, and Virginia. At need, they could help each other, however much they differed in religion, politics, and backgrounds. True, they were in some danger of French attack from Canada, but only in the summer. Deep snows would defeat any foe. To the south, however, Carolina was in as constant danger from Spanish and French attack as she had been in 1671, when Governor Sayle had written, "The Spanyard watcheth onely to destroy us."

Thousands of Indians who could be stirred into war by an enemy had been kept fairly friendly and peaceful by the trade established by Dr. Henry Woodward. Carolina's first great fortunes in the fur trade were the result of honest dealings with the Indians and the high quality of English trade goods. Yet this same trade, and the white men's steady encroachment on Indian lands would come nearer to wiping out the province than any attacks by European enemies.

By 1715, the Indian trade was Big Business. It was regulated by a Board of Indian Commissioners, whose records may still be read. Under them were agents, responsible, often important men, who lived among the Indians, often had Indian wives, and did their best to keep the natives from being cheated. They also kept alert to rumors of trouble.

The agents supervised licensed traders, whose headquarters were warehouses along the paths leading to Charles Town. Here, they received the furs and deerskins and traded tools, beads, cloth, brass kettles, English clothing— and guns, ammunition, and liquor. No Indian had tasted alcohol before the white men's coming. The traders' rum and whisky often drove them wild. The combination of firearms and firewater sparked many a massacre later.

Carolina's first large-scale Indian war, a curtain-raiser for the life-and-death struggle that followed, began in 1711, when the Tuscarora Indians of what was coming to be called North Carolina went on the warpath.

By 1653, a trickle of Virginia settlers had colonized parts of northeastern Carolina. Her guaranteed religious liberty continued to attract foreign settlers. In 1709, Baron Christopher de Graffenried and Louis Michel got a grant of ten thousand acres for French-speaking Swiss colonists from Berne, who settled on the Neuse River and called their town New Berne (Newbern). In surveying this grant, de Graffenried and John Lawson, surveyor-general of Carolina, strayed into Tuscarora Indian country. Mistaking this for a trick to have them give away more of their lands to the English, the Tuscaroras caught the men and tortured Lawson to death. On September 22, 1711, twelve hundred Tuscaroras attacked the New Berne Swiss, the Huguenots at Bath, and settlements along the Roanoke River. The three-day massacre ended only when the Indians were too drunk and exhausted to go on.

Deputy Governor Hyde, of North Carolina, called on Charles Town for help. Promptly, the Assembly voted £4,000 for arms and troops. By January 22, 1712, Col. John

Barnwell's white militia and friendly Indians had marched through hostile country and killed more than three hundred Tuscaroras at New Berne. Exhausted, short of provisions and with their commander wounded, the South Carolinians turned back—only to have the Tuscaroras start fighting again. In a few months, another force under Col. James Moore whipped the Indians so soundly that they left North Carolina and joined their Iroquois cousins in New York.

Carolinians had long considered the Yamassee Indians their friends. After the Spaniards had killed several Yamassee chiefs, the tribe had moved into the country around Port Royal. From there, they had raided Spanish settlements in Florida and tortured their prisoners so terribly that the Assembly had offered the Yamassees £5 reward for each Spaniard brought alive to Charles Town. The prisoners were then sent to St. Augustine.

Certainly, Beaufort Town (now Beaufort) on Port Royal River, would not have been founded in Yamassee country if any fears about the Indians' loyalty had been felt.

In 1715, however, the Yamassees began acting strangely. Traders noticed that they returned from Florida with new guns, ammunition, and colorful Spanish clothing. The traders refused to worry, however, because they thought they understood the Indians.

John Fraser, a Scottish trader living near Beaufort, got the first warning of trouble from his Yamassee friend, Sanute, who told him that the Bloody Stick, the war summons, was being sent around to every tribe in Carolina by the Yamassees. Sanute urged Fraser and his family to flee to Charles Town, offering them his own canoe if theirs was not large enough. Fraser tried to warn his neighbors before he left, but nobody believed him.

Governor Craven, however, took the rumors seriously.

The Yamassees raise the Bloody Stick

He sent Capt. Thomas Nairne, agent for Indian Affairs, John Wright, a prominent trader, and other responsible men to the Yamassee town of Pocotaligo, a few miles from Beaufort. There, they met the chiefs and discussed the Indians' complaints.

Nairne and Craven knew that the Yamassees resented the harshness of some traders towards the Indians. The bearers who carried heavy packs of skins many miles to Charles Town were often badly paid. Other traders had mistreated their Indian wives. Still others had allowed the Indians so much credit for trade goods that it was impossible for them to pay the total bills. (If the traders died, thought the Yamassees, who would know how much the Indians owed?) Chiefs and agents had a friendly talk, a feast and a drink, and the Englishmen went to bed thinking all was well.

At daybreak, April 15, 1715, the massacre began. One of several eyewitness accounts gives terrible details of the agents' death by torture. The traders' wives and children were murdered, too. In Pocotaligo and on nearby plantations more than ninety settlers were slaughtered.

Seaman Burroughs, a captain of the militia, dashed through a mob of Indians and swam a mile of river, though bullets pierced his neck and back. Running ten miles to the nearest settlement, he gave the alarm which spread to nearby plantations.

One band of Yamassees crossed the Combahee River and massacred one hundred settlers. Another party made for Beaufort, but Burroughs' warning had given people a chance to head for the harbor where a ship was anchored. Nearly four hundred terrified refugees swarmed aboard her and she set sail before the Indians could get near her. They burned the vacant plantation houses and shot the livestock.

Governor Craven was on his way to a conference with the Yamassees when news of the uprising reached him.

Appointing Maj. Robert Daniell as his deputy in Charles Town, he sent word to Col. Alexander Mackay to gather every available man and meet Craven at Pocotaligo. With 240 militiamen, Craven reached a spot only sixteen miles from the Indians' town, where he received word that Mackay had captured Pocotaligo and a neighboring fort, with the loss of only one man.

North of Charles Town, 400 Indians swooped down on Goose Creek Parish and most of the inhabitants fled to the city. Those who stayed to defend their homes were slaughtered. Within a very few miles of Charles Town, on June 13, Capt. George Chicken and his Goose Creek militia managed to stop the rush of the Yamassees.

With the governor and Assembly in emergency session, refugees poured into the town with grim news. The country was deserted for twenty miles around Charles Town. Crops rotted in the fields, houses were blackened ruins, dead cattle lay in the pastures. With no outside supplies Charles Town was faced with famine. Word came that every trader among the Apalachees, Creeks, Yamassees, Alabamas, and Choctaws had been murdered. Only the Chickasaws and Cherokees had protected the traders among them.

No real defense against all the Indians was possible. There were 10,000 Indians in the province and only 1,400 to 2,000 white men capable of bearing arms. The conspiracy to drive the English from the land extended from North Carolina's Cape Fear River to St. Augustine.

By September, the country around Charles Town was a nest of snipers. An old letters explains:

> They [the Indians] pursue their old method of Bush fighting & one or another of our Scouts are daily shot down without ever seeing an enemy. The Indians lye perdue [hidden] where they have learned some of our people will

pass. Or near some good Spring and being hidden by the bushes pour in their Volley and then scour off into the woods, so two or three men are killed and nobody did it. . . .

"Two or three" sounds like very little, but Carolina's population in 1715 was 6,200 whites and about 10,500 slaves.

"We are in hopes His Majesty will aid us," continued the letter, dated September 10, 1715, "for should this province be lost and the French settle it with the assistance of the Enemy, Virginia, New England and the whole English settlements would be exposed to very great danger."

This danger was ill-understood in the northern colonies. A Carolina agent, sent to Boston to buy six hundred muskets, was coolly treated and prompt cash payment demanded —though he got the guns. Virginia offered men and arms, but demanded a high price. Grateful North Carolina wasted no time in sending aid. A circle of forts on abandoned plantations ringed the province's small area of civilization, skirmishes went on, agents were sent to England to ask the Proprietors' help and, later, the king's.

The Proprietors dodged their responsibilities with neat excuses, though they did send a small shipment of arms. (They also asked that the back land rents be paid.) In London, the Commissioners for Trade and Plantations were told by the Carolina agents that even if troops were sent, food for at least one year must accompany them, since no new crops had been planted during the uprising. Letters from the province pointed out that Carolina's cash value to the Crown, in naval stores, rice, hides, and lumber showed that she was well worth saving.

On June 12, 1716, "An Address to the King's Most Excellent Majesty" from the Carolina Assembly gave one of the first hints of the coming revolution against the Proprietors. After citing the plight of the province, burdened with debts and on the verge of starvation, the petition ended with these words:

> Under these sad Circumstances, Great Sir, give us the representatives of the Province leave unanimously to Throw our Selves under Your Majesty's immediate Protection, under whose Care alone (under God) we can be Protected and Redressed and therefore begg your Most Sacred Majesty to grant our humble Request that this once Flourishing Province may be Added to those already under your happy Protection and which we are Assured will be of great Consequence for the Preservation of the Adjoyning Colonies and the increase of Your Majesty's Revenues.

Actually, the desperate Carolinians must have wondered just what help they *could* expect from fifty-six-year-old George I, born in Hanover, speaking only German, who had occupied the British throne just two short years. His claim to that throne was doubtful. England had crowned him only because he was Protestant, while his Stuart cousins, the previous kings, had been Catholic. Carolina's Lords Proprietors failed to foresee that the province they had founded would soon snatch self-government from their selfish hands and trust it to this unknown German king whose ministers were still as British as the Carolinians themselves. That action would shape the future course of Carolina's history.

Meanwhile, the war dragged on. The traders had lost £10,000 in Indian debts and the province's war debt had reached £140,000. Before the war, the total value of Carolina—stock, merchandise, houses, and lands—had been only £709,763. Indians were pressing to a very few miles of Charles Town. Governor Craven, marching against the hostile Cheraws and Catawbas to the north, had been recalled to the capital by news that seven hundred Apalachees from near the Savannah River had broken through the southern outposts and were looting plantations only a few miles from Charles Town.

A guard ship from Virginia arrived, with men, guns, and ammunition. North Carolina troops marched into Charles Town. This eased the danger, but nobody knew what the Cherokees were planning. Maurice Moore, a skilled Indian fighter, with three hundred North and South Carolina troops, marched into Cherokee country, to find that the Catawbas were urging them to war. After hearing Moore's arguments, the Cherokees turned on the Catawba messengers, killed them, and agreed to help the English in their fight against the troublemaking Creeks of what was later Georgia. French agents among the Creeks were prodding them to go on the warpath.

Not until 1717 did the war end. The Yamassees moved to Florida, where church bells rang welcome and cannon boomed salutes as the tribe entered St. Augustine. From that moment, they became bitter enemies of the Carolinians and would harass the province for years to come.

Now Carolina was safe—by land. By sea, she was threatened by a plague of pirates which she must deal with, alone.

chapter ten

 *A Plague of Pirates*

We think of pirates as seagoing gangsters, looting peaceful ships and forcing defenseless passengers to walk the plank. This idea is correct up to a point, but under certain conditions, piracy had long been legal in the 1700s.

Few nations had large navies. Instead, the kings depended on ships owned by captains who loaned them out in time of war, to harass the enemy's shipping. A commander with a few cannon aboard his ship got a Letter of Marque and Reprisal—a warrant to wage sea war—from his sovereign. From then on, whatever prizes he took were his. These legal pirates were called privateers.

American waters had swarmed with privateers and pirates since Spain's Silver Fleet had begun carrying treasure back to a land almost continually at war with England, Holland, and France. Often, privateers attacked and took cities as well as ships.

From Charles Town's beginning, the nearby waters had

swarmed with English privateers. The first Carolinians had welcomed this ready-made navy. As the town grew, the sea rovers would land and spend money freely. Their captured gold and silver pieces were almost the only real money in the province. They sold captured cargos cheap in Charles Town's streets. Thus, the city saw nothing wrong in giving the privateers safe harbor and entertainment, since they had robbed the right people.

In 1713, peace came briefly to Europe, releasing for private warfare thousands of men in the habit of looting and killing. Many became pirates. By 1715, at least eight hundred of them had seized the island of New Providence (near Andros) in the Caribbean and made it their base of operations along the Atlantic coast. The buccaneers' favorite refuge was the Cape Fear River and many coastal inlets in North and South Carolina. No shipping in their path was safe.

In 1715, Governor Craven had asked the Proprietors and the British government for help against these pirates who were capturing outgoing ships with rich cargos of rice and keeping vessels with needed British goods from entering the harbor. The Proprietors said they could do nothing. The British government refused to act unless the Proprietors returned the province to the king. In 1717, when Governor Robert Johnson renewed the plea, England was at war and needed all her ships. The king issued a proclamation pardoning all pirates who would stop raiding and swear allegiance to Great Britain. The pirates swore, lay low for a few months, and then resumed their raids. An expedition sent to New Providence to clean them out merely chased them north towards Charles Town. The Indian war was still bleeding Carolina of men and money. Now the province was faced with enemies at sea.

In early June, 1718, Edward Thatch (sometimes called Teach), a pirate nicknamed Blackbeard for his great bush

Edward Thatch—Blackbeard

of inky whiskers, appeared off Charles Town. His forty-gun ship was accompanied by three sloops and a total force of four hundred men. Thatch captured the pilot boat at the bar, and within a few days seized eight or nine ships bound for Europe. Aboard one was Samuel Wragg, a wealthy member of the provincial Council, his four-year-old son, William, and several other citizens of Charles Town.

Thatch needed medicines. He sent a message to the governor in Charles Town that unless the drugs were sent immediately, the heads of Wragg and his fellow passengers would be delivered to the town.

To save the prisoners and Charles Town, the governor and Council moved cautiously. By land, the city was quite defenseless. A hurricane in 1713 had swept away the walls

built by the governor's father, Sir Nathaniel Johnson. The
harbor was unprotected, for there was no armed, friendly
ship within hundreds of miles. The Indian war had almost
bankrupted Carolina, so no money was available to arm the
merchant ships still in harbor. Seething with helpless rage,
the citizens were under stern orders not to attack the pirates who swaggered through the streets.

Thatch got his medicines—and £1,500 in coin from
Wragg alone. Stripped almost naked, the prisoners were
left on a sandbar in the harbor while Thatch sailed safely
away.

Since Thatch was also raiding Virginia waters, an expedition hunted him down in 1718 and returned to port with
Blackbeard's head swinging from the lead ship's bowsprit.
Meanwhile Stede Bonnet, as feared as Thatch, was ravag-
ing the Carolina coast. In August, 1718, Bonnet, finding
his ten-gun, sixty-man sloop, the *Royal James*, needed repairs, hid up the Cape Fear River. To get timbers, Bonnet's men captured a shallop and broke her up. News of
the shallop's capture came to Charles Town.

Again, no British ships were at hand. Col. William Rhett,
the wealthy receiver-general of the province, got Governor
Johnson's permission to fit out two ships at his own expense
and hunt Bonnet down. On September 10, 1718, Rhett,
aboard the *Henry* with eight guns and seventy men, and
accompanied by the *Sea Nymph*, eight guns and sixty men,
moved out to Sullivan's Island for final preparations before
sailing for Cape Fear.

Just then, a sloop from Antigua came in, reporting that
another pirate, Charles Vane, with a twelve-gun brigantine
and ninety men, had stopped and robbed the sloop and let
her go, but had captured two other ships bound for Charles
Town. Vane had also intercepted two London-bound ships,
the *Neptune*, sixteen guns, and the *Emperor*, ten guns.

Though Rhett was now outgunned, he gave chase to Vane, only to have the pirate escape.

Rhett turned north in pursuit of Bonnet and the *Royal James*. On September 26, he entered the Cape Fear River and saw ahead the masts of Bonnet's ship. The tide turned, leaving Rhett's small vessels stuck on a sand bar at the river's mouth. The victory would go to the ship that first floated free.

At sunrise, Rhett saw the sails of the *Royal James* unfurled, heard the rattle of her anchor chains, and felt the breeze blowing straight away from the land. Down the river towards the ocean sped the pirate ship, with a running cannon fire as she came. Only the *Henry* was in position to fire back. The *Sea Nymph* was aground some distance off. For five hours, cannon roared in the Cape Fear until the *Henry* floated free. Skillfully aiming his sloop, Rhett forced the *Royal James* aground again. The pirate crew, seeing the fight was hopeless, forced Bonnet to surrender. The buccaneers were carried to Charles Town for trial.

The captured pirates were promptly tried before Justice Nicholas Trott, convicted, and hanged on White Point, now the site of Charles Town's Battery. Buried below highwater mark, their bones lie today under the trees and flowers of a quiet city park.

Carolina had won a sea fight against a force greater.and fiercer than the French-Spanish expedition of 1706. She had done it with no help from Proprietors or mother country. Now she found herself angry at the way she had been left alone, to survive or perish.

The London agent for the province was told to appeal to Parliament to have Carolina taken from the Proprietors and placed directly under the British Crown. This move got nowhere for three whole years.

Meanwhile, the Proprietors, with the aid of some Carolinians, sent over a list of "Instructions" designed to tighten their hold over their rebellious province. Many necessary acts of the Assembly were declared illegal. The Assembly itself was declared illegally elected. In despair, the governor

The citizens were delighted by the capture of the swaggering pirates

tried to ease the situation. He failed, and the people simply went ahead without him.

On November 28, 1719, Governor Johnson received a letter telling him that an association, composed of almost the entire population of South Carolina, was prepared to take over the government but would be glad to have him act as governor under the king. Johnson could only reply that he held his authority from the Proprietors and must obey them.

When the new Commons House of Assembly met, they informed the governor that the Proprietors might consider them illegally elected, but that they represented South Carolina and were assuming the government of the province until King George's wishes were known. Again they offered Johnson the governorship; again he declined. The Assembly then appointed James Moore as governor. For the first time, Carolinians had taken the government into their own hands.

Learning that the French and Spanish were planning another attack on Charles Town, Johnson wrote to the Assembly, begging them to allow him to conduct Charles Town's defense. He received no answer to his letter.

Just then, two British warships, the *Flamborough* and the *Phoenix* entered the harbor—a little late for fighting pirates, the reason they had been sent. The *Flamborough*'s captain recognized nobody but Johnson as governor, and prepared to enforce his orders. But Moore, the new governor, manned the seventy guns of Charles Town's bastions with five hundred fighting men and Johnson ordered the warships to withdraw.

Carolina had won her first revolution. In London, the king bought the Proprietors' shares of the province and South Carolina became a royal province, governed by king and Parliament directly from London.

 *Carolina Learns*

In the midst of wars and dangers, Carolina still provided her people with the means of learning.

In 1698, the first free publicly supported library in America was founded at Charles Town. Dr. Thomas Bray, who had started many religious libraries in the colonies, gave a collection of books, which the Assembly promptly took over, adding many volumes on general subjects and, on one occasion, sending a London bookseller the equivalent of $900 for more volumes. By 1724, so many books had been borrowed from this free library and not returned that the library almost disappeared!

Schools were considered next. In 1709, there were perhaps five hundred white children in the province. Many had doubtless been taught by their parents to read from the Bible (often the only book the family owned) and to write with fire-blackened sticks on bark or a clean shingle. But in 1700, John Lawson, surveyor-general of Carolina, recorded that the settlers "have Tutors among them that educate their youth à la mode [in the latest fashion]." In 1710 and 1712, however, the Assembly passed laws "for founding and erecting a free-school in Charles Town for the use of the inhabitants of South Carolina." The 1712 law added that "several well-disposed Christians, by their last wills have given several sums of money for the founding of a free-school."

Tax-paid education, free to everyone, was a very new idea. Parents had always paid to have their children taught in private schools or by tutors. The child whose family could not afford this went unschooled—though often such people learned to read somehow, and educated themselves surprisingly well.

The Carolina free-school law set up a commission on education composed of some of the most important men in the province. The commissioners were to take charge of the money willed for schools, add public funds to it, and see that schools were built and staffed with teachers "for the instruction of youth in grammar and other arts and sciences, and also in the principles of the Christian religion."

The teacher, who must be "capable of teaching the Greek and Latin languages" was to receive £100 a year—from the public treasury. This salary was about the same as an expert blacksmith's, and blacksmiths were among the highest paid workers in Carolina. The teacher had his house rent free and the use of the school house and the land around it. The free-school law also provided for "the support of an usher [assistant teacher] and a master to teach writing, arithmetic, merchants accompts [bookkeeping], surveying, navigation and practical mathematics." Twelve poor students were to be taught free. The others paid £4 to learn subjects which would enable them to earn their living in shipping or as planters.

More students studied Latin than Greek. The best books on medicine, law, history, philosophy, and science were still in the Latin in which they had been written. Translations were rare and books were still being written in Latin so that educated people anywhere could read them.

Even before the free-school law, worried parents had appealed for help to the Society for the Propagation of the Gospel in Foreign Parts, the missionary branch of the Church of England. While all Carolinians might worship as they chose, the Anglican (Episcopal) Church was the established, or state, church just as in England.

The society sent books and missionary teachers who set up schools in connection with the churches. In 1711, the first free church school in Charles Town was established in St. Philip's parish. In most church schools, the minister was also the teacher—luckily for the pupils, since Anglican clergymen had usually attended great British universities.

The missionary teachers were required "to take especial care of the manners of the pupils in and out of school; warning them against lying, falsehood and evil-speaking; to learn truth and honesty, to be modest, just and affable; to receive in their tender years that sense of religion which may render it the constant principle of their lives and actions."

Ties with England were still strong, and many parents still sent their children abroad to be educated. Little boys might be placed in school at the age of eight or ten and not see home again until they were in their late teens. Some studied at English, Scottish, and Irish universities, but more studied law in London because they knew they were the leaders of tomorrow and must know how to guide their province. These men's familiarity with English law aided Carolinians in their fight against oppression and later in helping to write the Constitution. Of the 114 Americans

A South Carolina classroom

admitted to practice law in London alone between 1759
and 1795, forty-three were South Carolinians.

Many Charles Town societies (most of them still in exist-
ence) opened free schools. The earliest was that founded
by the South Carolina Society in 1737.

No school, however, could teach the people of this new
country all they needed to know. They must learn by doing. A boy going into a trade or business was often appren-
ticed to a master craftsman or successful merchant, in whose
family he lived as he learned.

The planter's son's training was complicated and life-long. The future owner of a little kingdom of fields to be cleared, swamps to be ditched and drained, crops to be planted, tended, gathered, stored, and sold, must be master of every process on his plantation.

A rice planter had to be both surveyor and engineer. He had to know how to lay out and supervise the building of thousands of yards of dykes, or banks, between his fields and the swamps and rivers, since water had to flood the rice at certain times and be drawn off at others. The "trunks," or floodgates in the banks had to be kept in constant repair, otherwise the delicate rice plants suffered and the crop was lost. A foreman and overseer might help the planter—but only up to a point.

If the main crop was indigo, on the lighter, higher soils, it was the planter alone who must understand the chemical process of extracting dye from a brew of rotting plants and adding limewater at just the right moment. Ten minutes' bungling could spoil three months of work.

Once the crops were gathered and stored, the master had to turn bookkeeper, for crop values rose and fell with supply, demand, and the British trade laws. The plantation owner owed much to the "factor," the planter's Charles Town business representative, who sold the crops and collected the money, did the plantation shopping in town or abroad, and even loaned money in bad years. Faulty bookkeeping could mean ruin for a planter.

Often, the planter was the only available doctor. For this reason, many Carolinians studied medicine abroad and later in this country, though often they did not practice beyond their own districts. With simple surgical instruments, a "tooth-drawer" and a chest of medicines made up by Charles Town physicians, planters dealt with illness and accident in the home or in the slave quarters. The first native-born American to receive a European medical degree was William Bull, of Ashley Hall Plantation, who graduated from the University of Leyden in 1734. He would serve as acting governor of South Carolina for five terms between those of the last royal governors of the province.

The planter's wife had to be as accomplished as he was. She must train and manage the house servants, just as her husband taught his black carpenters, cattlemen, stable hands, boat makers, and field hands. The mistress supervised the weaving women, cooks, laundresses, candle makers, maids, gardeners, and nurses for her children. She was the head of the plantation "sick house," the infirmary. From her family recipe books she prepared herb remedies, soaps, and many things we buy in drug stores now. She was on call day and night in emergencies. She trained her daughters to follow in her ways, as her husband trained his sons. All this was a lifelong education.

 *The Rise of the Back Country*

Robert Johnson, commissioned in 1717, was the last governor under the Proprietors. Johnson divided the province into North and South Carolina, each with its own governor. Seeing that the white population of South Carolina had grown very slowly, and was far outnumbered by the Negroes, he realized that more white settlers must be brought in quickly. He therefore planned a chain of settlements, called townships, for the interior of the province and along rivers leading to Charles Town. The new settlers would fill up this territory, where there were few whites and also be a living fortification against the French and Indians.

The townships consisted of townsites and surrounding farmlands. The head of each settler family would receive a lot and fifty acres of farmland for himself, fifty more for each member of the family and fifty more for each servant. Money and livestock were offered, too. The townships were Kingston, on the Waccamaw; Queensboro, on the Peedee;

Williamsburgh on Black River; Fredericksburgh, on the Wateree; Amelia, on the Santee; Saxe Gotha, on the Congaree; Orangeburgh (Orangeburg), on the Edisto; and New Windsor and Purrysburgh, on the Savannah.

Purrysburgh, named for its founder, Jean Pierre Purry, of Neufchatel, Switzerland, was peopled by 152 Swiss at first, and more later, all specialists in silk culture. The mountain-born Swiss found the low, steamy climate unhealthy and soon scattered to other settlements.

Orangeburgh, on the Waccamaw, was settled by German-speaking Swiss, who made excellent farmers on the higher, fertile land. Amelia, on the Santee, named for the prettiest daughter of George II, was soon filled with Virginians, English, and Germans, along with the Huguenot planters who had been there a long time. Saxe Gotha was a German settlement; New Windsor, German-Swiss. Williamsburgh was a "Scotch-Irish" settlement made up of Presbyterian Scots who had fled to Ireland to escape religious persecution, and thence to the New World. Welsh Baptists settled on the Peedee, and more Virginians, Pennsylvanians, and some Irish Quakers took up land near Fredericksburgh. Thus, the Back Country was filled by people very different from the English and Barbadians near Charles Town.

With no large money crop like rice, the Back Country or Up Country people needed no droves of slaves. Hardworking, stubbornly independent, they produced almost everything they needed. They grew hemp for rope, flax, and cotton for clothing which was dyed with indigo and brews of barks and roots. Almost everyone kept sheep for meat and wool. Herds of cattle multiplied. The settlers grew big crops of fine wheat and corn, grinding the grain in mills built along the swift streams of the Up Country.

The first log cabins with their dirt floors and windows of greased paper soon gave way to big, plain, comfortable homes like Walnut Grove plantation near Spartanburg,

Walnut Grove plantation

which now looks much as it did when it was built in the
1760s. On the other hand, some settlers continued to oc-
cupy their simple cabins, adding to them as families grew.

By the 1760s, Up Country people were bringing their
surplus crops to Charles Town over wagon roads little better than trails. The covered wagons were drawn by as many
as eight horses, for mud holes were deep. The trip might
last for weeks until the men and boys arrived in the cap-

ital and parked their wagons in yards provided by Charles Town merchants. There, they traded hemp, butter, tallow, beef, wax, tobacco, and wool for salt, sugar, imported English tools, and a few luxury items. One thing, however, they seemed never to want—British tea.

Up Country people kept much to themselves in Charles Town. Its gay life, its fine buildings, its ladies and gentlemen dressed in silks and velvets, were like another world. Almost as though they had entered a foreign land whose language they could not speak, the Up Country people left Charles Town as soon as possible, without regret.

In 1733, a new colony, Georgia, was carved from South Carolina's territory. James Edward Oglethorpe and his 125 settlers landed in Charles Town where they were received with every kindness. William Bull accompanied the settlers to Yamacraw Bluff, on the Savannah River, and there helped lay out the city of Savannah. The Assembly gave the Georgians £8,000 and individuals contributed more money and much livestock.

With North Carolina carved from her northern boundary and Georgia from territory south of the Savannah River, South Carolina was left a small, triangular state. People seem not to have regretted this loss of territory at the time —it was that much less land to defend. Besides, in the little semicircle of parishes around Charles Town lay the visible wealth of South Carolina, in shipping, in culture, in activity. Sometimes it seemed as though the Low Country forgot that the Up Country was part of the same province. Part of this was due to the natural shortsightedness of people who were still busy repairing the damages of the Indian wars. Part was also due to the great distances and bad roads between the coast and the Up Country. In great measure, part was due to the innate difference in the people of the two sections and the resentment and suspicion that grew up in the Up Country against Charles Town.

Carolina's Up Country was in many respects very like the Old West. The same kind of pioneers were carving homes from the wilderness and fighting off Indians, combining to help each other build houses, plant crops, and round up livestock. The only courts were in the provincial capital, Charles Town. When outlaws from neighboring colonies swooped down upon the Back Country, stealing stock, robbing and killing settlers, there were no courts to try them—even if they had been caught—as they seldom were, at first. Thus, the sturdy settlers who had been brought into the townships that were to guard Low Country Carolina found themselves defenseless to try criminals unless they took them down to Charles Town.

As in the Old West, the Up Country people organized vigilante bands, called "Regulators." Losing no time, they rounded up thieves and murderers, burned the houses where they took refuge, and horsewhipped them the first time, dealing with the offenders much more severely for a second offense. When some of these outlaws went to Charles Town and sued the Regulators for their injuries, the Back Country people were furious. Violence broke out many times and only in 1772, when courts were finally established in the Back Country did the pioneers quiet down. They had also protested that they did not have enough representation in the Assembly, which was limited to only fifty members. The Carolinians of the Low Country were unwilling to give up any seats in the Assembly, pointing out that, for a hundred years they and their fathers had governed Carolina. But the Up Country people, who had been there only a few years, wanted equal representation.

Bitterness between the two sections of the province grew, as hot words flew between the settlers in the hills and the plantation owners on the coast. Right on the eve of the Revolution, South Carolina would find herself still divided at the moment of her deadliest danger.

The kitchen at Walnut Grove

chapter thirteen

The Darling of the Crown

In less than a century, the swampy peninsula ending in a sand flat had become one of the loveliest, busiest, wealthiest, and gayest cities in America.

Parts of Charles Town looked then much as they do today. Narrow streets, often paved with the smooth ballast stones that had steadied ships across the Atlantic were lined with tall houses whose ranks of piazzas, a West Indian invention, were swung to catch the ocean breezes that came with the tides and cooled the city. Most of the buildings were of gray-brown, native brick.

Tile-roofed, turned gable end to the streets, the houses, then as now, were shut in by high brick walls and lacy ironwork gates, through which one glimpsed gardens planted with rare flowers and shrubs from all over the world. The marble steps of those homes, the window glass and hardware might be imported. Inside, however, the exquisite cypress panelling and carving were apt to be the work of craftsmen trained in London who had come to Carolina and spent the rest of their lives there.

Charles Town's elegant mahogany furniture was often made locally by cabinet makers like Thomas Elfe (1719–75). His still existing account books show that in eight years alone he turned out 1,502 items, ranging from giant library bookcases like that in the Heyward-Washington house to tables, chairs, beds, even carved picture frames. Elfe imported mahogany planks and logs from the West Indies.

Much fine silver was locally made, too. The town had plenty of craftsmen capable of making bowls, pitchers, tea sets, and goblets as beautiful as any produced abroad. These men also repaired watches, made clocks, and were skilled engravers.

In Charles Town houses hung portraits by such local

A library bookcase attributed to Thomas Elfe

artists as Henrietta Johnston (d. 1729), possibly America's first woman artist. Jeremiah Theus, whose father had come with the Swiss to Orangeburgh Township in the 1730s painted many portraits in Charles Town and vicinity where he worked for thirty-five years.

Thus, Charles Town was developing a native culture that, though linked with England's, was still her own.

Her weekly newspaper, the *South-Carolina Gazette,* established in 1731 by an editor who died a few months later, was taken over in 1734 by Lewis Timothy, sent to Charles Town by Benjamin Franklin. The *Gazette* became one of the liveliest journals in the colonies and would later be one of the most constant fighters for American liberty. When, in December, 1738, Timothy met death by accident, his widow, Elizabeth became our first newspaper woman by continuing publication until her son, Peter, was old enough to take over.

Peter Timothy became one of the firebrands of the Revolution, as the columns of the *South-Carolina Gazette* show. He published not only advertisements, and announcements of weddings and deaths, but essays and verse by Charles Town writers and also by New England patriots like James Otis.

Winter and summer, the town offered amusements and cultural advantages. The flooded rice fields of the plantations bred malaria-carrying mosquitoes that made the months from May to late October deadly for white men, though slaves, straight from Africa, seemed immune. Planters' families moved to Charles Town in summer. Family visits, parties, lectures, plays, and concerts helped pass the time until it was safe to return home. Winter was another busy time, since no crops were being raised. Planters brought their horses in for the races run in January and February. Prizes included silver cups, fine saddles, and embroidered waistcoats. Another brilliant season ended only with the beginning of Lent.

As early as 1704, Anthony Aston, an English player, had performed in Charles Town and had written "one play on the subject of the country." On January 24, 1735, the town's first real dramatic season began with the performance of *The Orphan, or the Unhappy Marriage,* by the English dramatist, Thomas Otway. The play was presented in the courtroom on the second floor of the Exchange, there being no regular theater in Charles Town. Here, too, in 1735, was presented the first musical play staged in this country, *Flora, or Hob in the Well,* by Colley Cibber, a brilliant London actor and writer of smash hits. In 1736, the Dock Street Theater opened with a performance of *The Recruiting Officer,* a farce by the Irish dramatist, George Farquhar.

Charles Town's musical activities are often shown in the columns of the *Gazette.* Notices of concerts by visiting musicians, sales of new music and instruments, and advertisements of people who tuned and repaired them are frequent. In 1762, America's oldest amateur musical society, the St. Cecelia, was founded in Charles Town.

The Charles Town Library Society, founded in 1748, possessed not only a large collection of books, magazines, and papers but also scientific apparatus, including a microscope, and rooms where visiting scientists lectured on electricity, the latest discoveries in chemistry, and scientific methods of farming. In 1773, the society invited Carolinians who possessed fossils or historical relics to deposit them with the society. Thus began the Charles Town Museum, oldest in this country. These facilities became a center for Carolinia scientists, of whom there were many even then. Perhaps the most remarkable was Dr. John Lining (d. 1760) who corresponded with Franklin, repeated his kite-and-key experiment in a Charles Town thunderstorm, wrote about his findings for European publications, and conducted the first scientific weather observations, with instruments, in this country. Dr. Lionel Chalmers also published weather

The making of indigo

observations from 1750 to 1756. Early South Carolina bot-
anists included Dr. Thomas Dale, Dr. Alexander Garden
for whom the gardenia is named, and many others. Charles
Town's botanical gardens were extensive and beautiful.

Rice and indigo produced the wealth that made all this
beauty and progress possible. Rice had been cultivated very
early, but British laws requiring that all such crops be
shipped directly to Great Britain had placed Carolina rice
growers at the mercy of London merchants who paid what
they pleased for the crop and resold it at high prices. In
1730, however, the law was changed to allow Carolina rice
to be shipped directly to any part of Europe south of Cape
Fenisterre, on the northwestern tip of Spain. This ruling
opened the whole Mediterranean world to Carolina rice.
Money poured into the province.

The indigo culture which, in the words of an early
historian, "proved equally profitable as the mines of Mexico

and Peru" began with experiments conducted by seventeen-year-old Eliza Lucas, on her father's plantation near Charles Town. Indigo had been a monopoly of growers in the French West Indies, so British weavers, dependent on them for blue dye, had to purchase it from their enemies. Great Britain was anxious to have indigo grown and prepared in her own territory. Eliza and her neighbor and helper, Andrew Devaux, had several failures but ultimately they produced dye that equalled that of the French. Carolina's production of indigo skyrocketed when Parliament, in 1748, granted a bounty, or subsidy of sixpence per pound on all the dye the province could produce. In 1774 and 1775, Carolina exported over one million pounds of indigo to Great Britain. Fortunes grew, for Great Britain was still paying that bounty at the time of the Revolution.

No wonder the province had a building boom that began in the 1740s! Along the great "rice rivers" of the Low

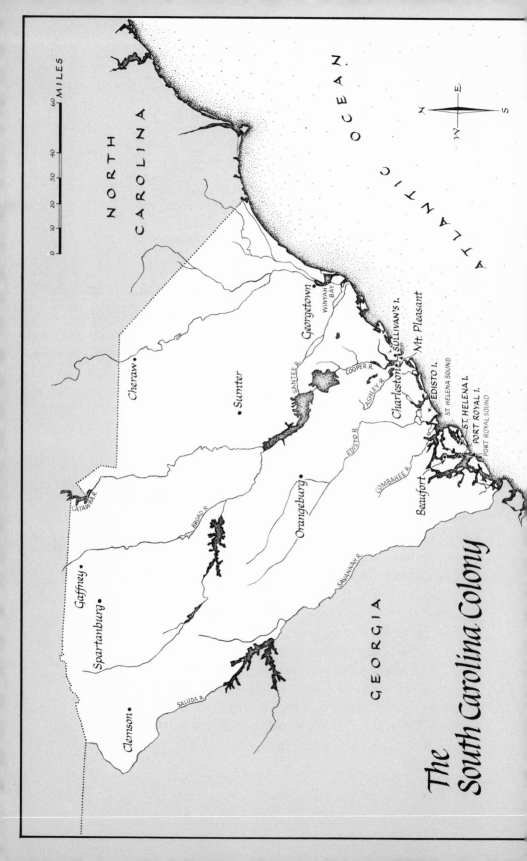

The
South Carolina Colony

Country, the grain flourished behind miles of river dykes. Far into the Back Country, indigo was raised, shipped down to Charles Town and thence to London. In Georgetown and Beaufort, as well as in Charles Town, churches, public buildings, and fine homes, many still standing, date from this time of prosperity.

Charles Town's stately, white St. Michael's Church, with clock, bells, font, and organ made in England, was completed in 1761. The Exchange, at the foot of Broad Street, the city's customhouse and trade center, dates from 1772. Such mansions as the Miles Brewton House at 27 King Street, completed in 1769 at a cost of £8,000, an enormous sum in those days, remain as evidence of the wealth that rice and indigo brought Carolina.

The elaborate coaches and fine horses, the beautiful clothing worn by the people are explained by Bostonian Josiah Quincy's diary. "The number of shipping," he wrote, "far surpasses all I had seen in Boston. I was told that there were not so many as common at this season, though about 350 sail lay off the town. . . ."

Three hundred and fifty ships, loading along the great "bridges" or wharves, projecting out into Cooper River! Barrels of rice and indigo, hides, lumber, naval stores, even a little cotton—no wonder rich factors and merchants could draw checks on bankers over most of Europe. In 1770, the Carolinas exported the equivalent of £1,250,000—and paid out only £650,000 in imports. It was a wonderful balance of trade. No wonder South Carolina was called "The Darling of the Crown."

In business, in peace, in beauty and prosperity, she had everything to lose by joining the Revolution. The war would stop the indigo bounty and bankrupt the planters, paralyze the rice industry, bottle up ships in harbor, and make her one of the chief battlegrounds of the Revolution.

One thing, however, she stood to gain—her liberty.

 *The Revolution Begins*

The French and Indian War had ended in 1763. Most of the conflict had taken place outside South Carolina, though the war had sparked a Cherokee uprising and produced bloody massacres in the Up Country. Finally, the Cherokees were conquered and driven back into the mountains. When France and England signed a peace treaty, England received all the country east of the Mississippi River except New Orleans. South Carolina received much of the old Cherokee country.

Settlers continued to pour into the Up Country, so that Charles Town was no longer an island of civilization in a wilderness. But the ill-feeling between the new Carolinians and the old ones continued. Up Country people felt that because they had no courts, few churches and schools, they were South Carolina's forgotten men. The Regulators still rode when robbery and murder threatened Up Country homes. Only in 1772 were courts established which made armed bands protecting the peace unnecessary. The Up Country, however, still fought for representation in the Assembly at Charles Town. The law, however, limited the number of members.

England, deeply in debt after the French and Indian war, felt that the colonies should pay part of the price of a conflict which had been fought in their defense. The Stamp Act was passed. A tax of only a few pennies on each sheet of paper used for legal purposes, newspapers, etc., seemed no hardship to anybody. (Indeed, such tax stamps on public papers are used in Europe to this day.) But in 1765, the colonies refused to use the stamped paper or even to receive it at their ports. They refused to be taxed by Parliament, in which they had no representation.

Great Britain's reasoning was that the colonies should bear a share of the expenses of an army raised to defend them. This was estimated at ten thousand men, to be stationed in the colonies. Every penny spent on maintaining this army would be spent in America. If the colonies could not be taxed to support such an army, then the expense must come from voluntary contributions by the colonial assemblies or from the people in England under the taxes imposed by Parliament. Were the colonies to enjoy the advantages of being part of the British Empire and pay nothing for the privilege?

The colonies, on the other hand, had no way of imposing a general uniform tax on all thirteen colonies, nor were they willing to be taxed from abroad.

When the stamped paper arrived in Charles Town on October 20, 1765, Acting Governor William Bull, well-known for his loyalty to the king as well as his love for the province, had the shipment stored at Fort Johnson, under heavy guard. For nine days Charles Town was filled with threats, fights, and searching of houses where the stamps might possibly be stored—for nobody knew where they were.

When Massachusetts called for a Stamp Act Congress to oppose the tax, South Carolina sent Thomas Lynch, a Georgetown planter, Christopher Gadsden, one of the first in the colony to call for independence, and John Rutledge, a brilliant lawyer and later the president of his state. The Stamp Act Congress sent Parliament its resolution of protest, which gained the sympathy of William Pitt, the great English statesman, who, on January 14, 1766, made a speech in Parliament.

"It is my opinion," Pitt thundered, "that this kingdom has no right to lay a tax upon the colonies!" Carefully, clearly he explained the limits of Parliament's power to tax. "Gentlemen," he added, "I have been charged with giving birth to sedition in America. They have spoken their sentiments with freedom against this unhappy Act, and that freedom has become their crime. . . . The gentleman [Lord Grenville, another speaker] tells us, America is obstinate; America is almost in open rebellion.

"I rejoice that America has resisted!"

Thanks largely to Pitt's efforts, the Stamp Act was repealed on March 18, 1766.

The repeal of the Stamp Act was celebrated by Christopher Gadsden and his Liberty Boys beneath Charles Town's Liberty Tree, a great live oak in a pasture just north of what is now Calhoun Street. After Gadsden's speech on the evils of tyranny, the Liberty Boys joined hands around the oak, swore to be faithful to American liberty—and then had lunch under the tree. (The British burned the oak when they captured the town.)

Most South Carolinians, however, hoped that separation from the mother country would not be necessary. Caro-

The colonists confront a stamp officer

linians felt their duty to the Crown deeply. Some leaders even wept at the idea of rebellion against Great Britain which was, after all, still the homeland of all Englishmen.

When the new royal governor, Lord Charles Greville Montagu, arrived in 1767, however, South Carolinians received a shock. Though Parliament had repealed the Stamp Act, it was determined to show the colonies who still held the whip hand. The governor's coming brought news of the Townshend Act, which taxed glass, paper, paint, lead, and tea imported into the colonies. Massachusetts promptly called for a protest against all such taxes, and while Governor Montagu tried to keep the Commons House of Assembly from ratifying the protest, he soon found himself helpless.

The colonies then joined in a general boycott of British products. They refused to buy British exports, and refused to sell products to England, too. They hoped that since England got most of the raw materials she needed for manufacturing from the colonies, she would be hurt by the boycott.

This Nonimportation Agreement among the colonies did hurt British manufacturing, but it also bankrupted merchants in America—because their shops grew empty of anything to sell. It encouraged smuggling—because goods had to come from somewhere. A Committee of Inspection

A handbill expressing support of the Non-Importation Agreement

The true Sons of Liberty

And Supporters of the Non-Importation Agreement,

ARE determined to rëfent any the leaft Infult or Menace offer'd to any one or more of the feveral Committees appointed by the Body at Faneuil-Hall, and chaftife any one or more of them as they deferve ; and will alfo fupport the Printers in any Thing the Committees fhall defire them to print.

σAS a Warning to any one that fhall affront as aforefaid, upon fure Information given, one of thefe Advertifements will be pofted up at the Door or Dwelling-Houfe of the Offender.

opened every parcel from Great Britain and if it contained goods for sale, it was seized and stored in warehouses rented for the purpose. The Nonimportation Agreement caused widespread unemployment in Great Britain. One speech in Parliament pointed out that just eight British merchants had lost £400,000 in cancelled orders from America.

Since the colonies had not yet learned to work together, the Nonimportation Agreement did not last long. By 1770, the agreement had been abandoned in all American ports except Charles Town. Only on May 30, 1771, did the *South-Carolina Gazette* report that British goods were coming in and that half-empty shops were beginning to fill with merchandise. Only tea was excepted. The colonies felt they had to draw the line somewhere.

Faced with the loss of so much trade, Parliament, in 1770, repealed all taxes on goods imported into the colonies except those on tea. The East India Company, which supplied tea to British merchants, was very near failure. British investors would lose money if the company went bankrupt. The Townshend Act had tried to help the East India Company by taking off the heavy tea tax collected in England and substituting a small tax of three pence per pound on all tea imported into the colonies. Thus, tea cost less in Charles Town than in London, where the heavy tax was still collected. The colonies were alert to such tricks, however, and the three-penny tea tax was soon making people angrier than the Stamp Act had done.

Peter Timothy, editor of the *South-Carolina Gazette*, kept his readers informed and indignant over the tea tax. He printed letters written locally and as far away as Massachusetts to show that this trifling tax on tea was Parliament's way of asserting its power to tax Americans without their consent. In the autumn of 1773, the East India Company, licensed to export more than half a million pounds of tea to America, sent ships to the four principal ports of the colonies—Boston, New York, Philadelphia, and Charles Town. The Charles Town tea went unclaimed by local merchants. At the end of twenty days it was lawfully seized and stored in the vaults under the Exchange at the foot of Broad Street.

On January 17, 1774, the *South-Carolina Gazette* carried the following news item from Massachusetts: "Some *Mohawks*, on the 16th ult. [of last month] hoisted out all the Chests that were on board Captain Hall's and Captain Bruce's Ships and Captain Coffin's Brig, cut them to pieces and threw the whole contents over the Sides into the water."

Such was Peter Timothy's account of the Boston Tea Party which had occurred December 16, 1773. News of the Tea Party reached London in March, 1774. Parliament promptly passed the Boston Port Act. The port of Boston was closed, Salem was made the seat of government, and Marblehead the port of entry for the former capital's food and supplies. The charter of Massachusetts was changed so that its people were powerless. A military governor was placed over the colony. With the port of Boston closed, its workers faced starvation.

Parliament's orders went into effect in Boston on June 1, 1774. When Charles Town heard of her neighbor's plight she reacted quickly, for the old tie between the two cities was warm and strong. More than two hundred barrels of rice were soon on the way to Boston, and money for relief was pouring in. The fund reached £3,300—more than that contributed by any other colony.

As tension mounted, families, friends, and business associates were divided in loyalty to the American cause—or the king's. Church of England clergymen found their congregations rebellious. When, on August 14, 1774, the Reverend John Bullman, assistant rector of St. Michael's Church in Charles Town delivered a sermon called "The Christian Duty of Peaceableness," the vestry dismissed him. At ancient St. James in Goose Creek Parish, the rector, Mr. Ellington, uttering the usual prayer, "that it may please Thee to bless and preserve our Sovereign Lord, King George" did not receive the customary "We beseech Thee to hear us, good Lord." Instead, from the depths of the high-walled pew occupied by Ralph Izard, came the loud response, "Good Lord, deliver us!"

When more tea shipments had come to Charles Town, they were turned back. On November 1, 1774, however, the ship *Britannia* anchored off Charles Town. Search of her cargo revealed that she carried a few small chests of tea consigned to several Charles Town merchants, one of whom, Zephaniah Kingsley, was aboard. The captain, Samuel Ball, had been absent from his ship when the tea was loaded. He convinced the Committee of Observation (which checked all cargoes) that he was innocent of "any design to counteract the Americans," as the *Gazette* explained. The committee then called in the men who had ordered and paid for the tea—Robert Mackenzie, Robert Lindsay, and Zephaniah Kingsley—and told them what they had to do. What followed was the Charles Town Tea Party, reported by Peter Timothy as follows:

> On Thursday at Noon [November 3, 1774] an Oblation was made to NEPTUNE, of the said seven Chests of Tea, by Messrs *Lindsay Kingsley* and *Mackenzie* Themselves, who going on board the Ship in the Stream [Cooper River] with their own Hands respectively stove the Chests belonging to each, and emptied their Contents into the River, in the Presence of the *Committee of Observation*, who likewise went on board, and in view of the whole General Concourse of People, who gave three hearty Chears after the emptying of each Chest, and immediately separated as if nothing had happened.

The same thing happened at Georgetown.

chapter fifteen

 *Preparing for War*

It was the Low Country that marshalled the sharply divided province towards rebellion, then independence, then war. Understandably, the Back Country was unwilling to join any war against George III.

Wasn't he German as were many of the settlers? Hadn't he given them these lands on which stood the houses they had built and defended from the Indians? The refugee French and Swiss had no quarrel with the monarch who had given them a new home. The Scotch-Irish must have shuddered as they recalled the last uprising in Scotland against a British king in 1745. Their lands had been confiscated, their families left to starve. Was all this to happen again—*here?* Who cared about taxes on tea that almost nobody drank?

On July 6, 1774, after news of the British occupation of Boston and the so-called Intolerable Acts against Boston and Massachusetts reached Charles Town, a mass meeting of citizens adopted a resolution condemning these acts of Parliament. They voted to send as delegates to the First Continental Congress, in Philadelphia, Henry Middleton, John and Edward Rutledge, Christopher Gadsden, and Thomas Lynch, Jr.

Meeting from September 5 to October 26, 1774, the Continental Congress addressed a loyal and dignified protest to King George, begging him to hear and remedy their grievances. They added a Declaration of Rights, claiming for Americans the ancient rights of Englishmen. They organized an association pledged not to import or export British goods as long as the "Intolerable Acts" were in force. If matters grew worse, they would meet again in May, 1775.

Both protest and Declaration of Rights were ignored by king and Parliament.

On January 11, 1775, the Provincial Congress was organized at a citizens' mass meeting in Charles Town. It was high time, for the province had been without representative government for three long years. In October, 1772, the royal governor, Lord Charles Grenville Montagu, had tried to make the Assembly obey him, and, when it refused, he adjourned it. By law, it could not reconvene until summoned by the governor. Since the province's earliest days, the Assembly, composed of two houses like a modern legislature, had governed Carolina under governors appointed by the king. Most governors had been honest, able men, but Lord Charles Grenville Montagu was not one of them. Leaving the already rebellious assembly powerless to meet, he had gone back to England in 1773, leaving William Bull as acting governor. Old, tired, far from well, Bull was torn between his loyalty to the king and his love for Carolina. His family, sadly divided now, had served the province with devotion and honor since the first of them, Stephen Bull, had landed in 1670.

The newly formed Provincial Congress asked Acting Governor Bull to reconvene the Assembly, since the affairs of the province were in disorder. Though this request came from a body composed of many of Bull's relatives, friends, and neighbors, the old man, still loyal to his king, ruled that the Provincial Congress was an illegal organization, so Bull could not hear their request. Only the next royal governor could reconvene the Assembly. Understanding the old man's position, the Congress went about its business without him .

The 184 members, with Charles Pinckney as president, passed resolutions recommending military training for all citizens and appointing February 17, 1775, as "a day of fasting, humiliation and prayer, before Almighty God, devoutly to petition Him to inspire their King with true wisdom, to defend the people of North America in their just title of freedom and to avert from them the impending calamities of civil war."

Civil War. This name was applied repeatedly to the conflict which only later would be called revolution. Gen. Willam Moultrie, in his *Memoirs of the American Revolution*; the historian, Dr. John Drayton, son of William Henry Drayton, a member of the Continental Congress from 1778 until his death in 1779; resolutions of the Provincial Congress, all use the term that meant a fight between brothers with an ocean between them, but brothers nonetheless.

Before adjourning, the Provincial Congress appointed a Committee of Five to "look after the defenses of the province and the safety of the people." William Henry Drayton, Arthur Middleton, Charles Cotesworth Pinckney (Charles Pinckney's cousin) , William Gibbes, and Edward Weyman (a leading Liberty Boy) soon had much to "look after."

On April 19, 1775, while guns were blazing at the Battle of Lexington, the ship *Swallow* arrived with English mail. Drayton and John Neufville, of the Nonimportation Committee, took the ship's mailbags from the postmaster and carried them to the State House for inspection. No private letters were opened. But in the mailbag were letters from Lord Dartmouth in London to Governor Dunmore, of Virginia; Governor Martin of North Carolina; Lord William Campbell, South Carolina's royal governor who had not yet arrived in the province; Governor Wright, of Georgia, and Governor Tonyne, at St. Augustine, Florida, a British possession since 1763. Opening these letters, the committee found they all said the same thing. King and Parliament were losing patience with these Americans. Gather men loyal to His Majesty's government and be ready. While Great Britain dislikes the use of force, this rebellion must and shall be crushed.

That same night, the Committee of Five and many of the town's leading citizens, decided to seize all powder, arms, ammunition, and equipment in British hands and to arm the miltia. Guns in patriots' hands meant safety for Charles Town and fewer weapons for future invaders. Powder in patriots' possession meant empty enemy cannon.

The next night, William Henry Drayton and his committee broke into the powder magazine on Charles Town Neck (the north end of the peninsula), removed the powder, and floated it downriver in boats to Christopher Gadsden's wharf and warehouse.

Another party rowed across the Cooper and Wando rivers which flow together just northeast of Charles Town and raided the powder magazine on Hobcaw Point. They found it empty. The royal powder receiver, Capt. Robert Cochrane, had removed the kegs and hidden them in nearby bushes. Later, when he reported them "stolen," nobody could prove otherwise. Shortly this powder was also in patriot hands.

The guns were stored in the attic of the State House, at the corner of Broad and Meeting streets. The city Guard

The old powder magazine in Charleston, dating from 1703

House was just across the way. Yet, on the night of April 21, 1775, nobody heard the big, wooden State House doors being forced open, nor the clank of metal as eight hundred muskets, two hundred cutlasses and much equipment were carried down several flights of stairs, out into the streets, and away. By dawn, everything was hidden in houses, cellars, and William Johnson's blacksmith shop, on the Bay. Old Acting Governor Bull, who had slept through the arms raid in his Meeting Street mansion three blocks away, offered a reward of £100 sterling for information or the guns' return. Nobody claimed the money.

Powder from just two magazines was far from enough. Learning that the brig *Betsy*, with one hundred barrels of

British powder, was bound for St. Augustine, another party in the sloop *Commerce* hurried south. It caught the *Betsy* while she waited for high tide to boost her over St. Augustine bar. The powder, transferred to the *Commerce*, was rushed to Beaufort, where small boats from Charles Town took off most of it. A boatload of strangers approached during the loading and explained that New England needed powder. The Carolinians gave them twenty barrels.

That was how British powder, meant to subdue the southern colonies, spat flames and death, instead, at the Battle of Bunker Hill.

The Second Continental Congress assembled in Philadelphia on May 10, 1775, voted to raise an army and appointed George Washington its commander-in-chief. News of Lexington and Concord reached Charles Town on May 8, but the Provincial Congress waited until June 1 to reassemble. The delay was meant to give members time to think calmly about what might lie ahead. Since most of the members of the Assembly were also members of the Congress, they took over the government of the province, ordered three regiments of militia to be formed, and voted £1,000,000 in paper money for defense. A thirteen-member Council of Safety was created with authority over troops and public money. On June 17, 1775, Col. William Moultrie was placed in command of the Second Regiment in the provincial service.

Next day, South Carolina's last royal governor, Lord William Campbell, arrived at Charles Town. No cheering crowds, military parades or cannon salutes greeted him. Finding himself a helpless shadow-governor, with the Provincial Congress in full control, Lord William got in touch with the Back Country Loyalists, whom the Congress had tried vainly to interest in joining the general revolt. Spies and messages came and went between Lord William and such Back Country Tory leaders as Moses Kirkland. When these activities were discovered, angry crowds began gathering before the house in which the governor was staying, threatening his safety.

On September 15, 1775, the governor, having dismissed the Assembly and issued a number of troublesome last orders, took the Great Seal of the province, without which no government acts were legal, and, with Kirkland, slipped into a boat on Vanderhorst's Creek, just back of the Meeting Street house. They were rowed out to the *Tamar*, a warship lying in the channel.

Royal government had ended in South Carolina.

 # Battle Flags Are Flying

The *Tamar* and the newly arrived *Cherokee* remained in the channel between Sullivan's Island and Charles Town, a nuisance to shipping and a threat to the town, should they move closer. Before he left, Lord William Campbell had ordered a party of wreckers to Fort Johnson, with instructions to throw the guns off their wooden carriages but not to damage them otherwise, since the returning British would need them.

The wreckers were gone only an hour or two before one hundred fifty picked men from the Second South Carolina Regiment, under Captains C. C. Pinckney, Bernard Elliott, and Francis Marion arrived at the fort in small boats, in the midst of a driving wind and rain. Clothing, ammunition, powder, and the matches (coils of rope that smoldered and could be carried some distance) were soaked. By daybreak three cannon had been remounted, loaded, and pointed at the two British ships—which promptly moved out of range. Over the fort was raised the first American flag displayed in South Carolina. Col. William Moultrie, in

William Moultrie

his *Memoirs*, tells how he designed the flag with its dark blue ground matching the color of the Second Regiment's uniform, and a white crescent in the upper right-hand corner.

King George declared the colonies in revolt and named all Americans in arms as traitors. American ships could be seized on the high seas as British prizes of war. Old historians like Dr. David Ramsay, who lived through the Revolution spoke bitterly of these rulings. Ramsay spoke of the rulings "confiscating American property and throwing all colonists out of His Majesty's protection." News of these rulings, which arrived in Charles Town in March, 1776, united people who had been slow to end their ties with Great Britain.

The Back Country, meanwhile, was close to civil war. Rumors spread that powder furnished to the Indians by traders (for hunting) was to be used in making war on the settlers. At one place, Loyalists were tarred and feathered. In another, Loyalists drove out those who had agreed to support the revolt. As time went on, many expert riflemen from the Back Country agreed to join the militia, and North Carolinians hurried down to join them. In the fights that followed, many Loyalists were captured and taken to

Charles Town, but all were released by the Council of Safety, which hoped thus to win the prisoners to the American cause. This action did win much respect for the Provincial Congress and lessen tension between the two parts of the province. By the end of 1775, the Back Country was almost ready for the Revolution. By the time that section had known the fury of British invasion, tough men in hunting shirts would be serving under Low Country commanders like Marion, or officers from beyond the Carolina border, like Nathaniel Greene. From Cowpens to King's Mountain their bullets would find their mark, harrying the invaders ever northward until they landed, exhausted, at Yorktown, ripe for surrender.

The province was still in confusion, with no governor, courts closed, and turmoil everywhere. It was the same in other colonies. The Continental Congress in Philadelphia advised several colonies, among them South Carolina, to frame new constitutions and set up their own governments until Great Britain saw reason.

A committee of eleven great Carolinians drafted the state Constitution of 1776. Among them were future signers of the Declaration of Independence and several who would assist in framing the Constitution of the United States. The eleven men were: Charles Cotesworth Pinckney and his cousin, Charles Pinckney; Henry Laurens, Christopher Gadsden, Rawlins Lowndes, Henry Middleton and his son, Arthur; Thomas Bee, Thomas Lynch, Jr., John Rutledge, and Thomas Heyward, Jr. On March 21, 1776, the Constitution of South Carolina went into effect. The Provincial Congress became the General Assembly of South Carolina. Brilliant, able John Rutledge was elected president.

With a constitution, the General Assembly as governing body, with new judges appointed, with a standing army and a president, South Carolina had become an independent republic one hundred days before the Declaration of Independence was proclaimed in Philadelphia on July 4, 1776.

chapter seventeen

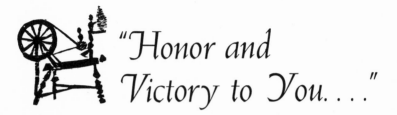

"Honor and Victory to You...."

Lord William Campbell, stranded aboard the *Tamar* while his wife remained in Charles Town, was busy causing the new South Carolina government as much trouble as possible. Both the *Tamar* and the *Cherokee*, still anchored awkwardly in Charles Town harbor, were demanding supplies of food and water from the mainland, but the General Assembly allowed this only from day to day. Meanwhile, Lord William wrote more letters to London which were taken out by ships that came and went beyond the range of Fort Johnson's guns.

"The interior is ready at any time to rise up against those in Charles Town who are promoting rebellion," wrote his lordship. "Three regiments, a proper detachment of artillery with a couple of good frigates, some small craft and a bomb-ketch [bomb throwing ship] will do the whole business here and go a long way to reduce Georgia and North Carolina to a sense of their duty. . . ."

Naturally, authorities in London who read such letters thought that an invasion of Charles Town would bring the three southern colonies quickly to their knees. A fleet was prepared in the north.

Batteries of heavy guns erected at Haddrell's Point (now Mt. Pleasant) on the night of December 19, 1775, drove the *Tamar* and *Cherokee* out past Sullivan's Island. A few days later, guns on the island forced them to sea. Two British warships had joined them, and these had made the patriots hurry to fortify Sullivan's Island as well as Charles Town. Nobody doubted that an attack would come. Lookouts north of the town were keeping watch for any fleets and would send "expresses"—fast riders—to warn Charles Town.

The city itself was on the alert. By Colonel Moultrie's orders and those of President Rutledge, crews of fire fighters were stationed throughout the southern part of the town, with squads manning fire engines. Fire marshals had orders that if a blaze was sighted anywhere in town, a long staff with a lantern on the end should be held out of the steeple of St. Michael's Church in the direction of the fire. The men in charge of the province's safety had, apparently, thought of everything.

With the *Tamar* and *Cherokee* gone, Charles Town could build forts where she chose. Cannon commanding the entrance to the channel at the harbor's mouth could shut out any enemy, while Long Island (now called the Isle of Palms) and Sullivan's Island lay open to attack.

It was decided to build a major fort on the western end of Sullivan's Island. There was no time to get together the usual materials of brick or tabby. No stone was available. The main idea was to mount as many guns as possible behind something and on something.

One thing was plentiful on the island—palmetto logs. Their spongy wood was easily cut, though nobody at the time dreamed of their absorbent qualities. Working around the clock, South Carolinians built a big, square fort of two layers of palmetto logs sixteen feet apart with hard-packed sand as filling. From each corner, bastions shaped like big Indian arrowheads jutted out with cannon mounted so as to make a deadly cross fire against the invaders. On one of them floated the dark blue crescent flag of South Carolina. The fort was big enough to contain one thousand men. But the back wall was not completed and there was a wide, marshy place in the middle. The fort mounted thirty-one cannon of different sizes.

On June 4, 1776, General Charles Lee, the expert sent by General Washington to take command of the South Carolina troops and arrange for the fort's defense, arrived. Lee had had bits and pieces of military experience abroad and claimed to know much more about fighting than he actually did. The Americans, however, were desperate for experienced officers and Lee was the best man Washington could spare just then. Moultrie called him "hasty and rough in his manners," but added that "he taught us to think lightly of the enemy." Lee called the log fort a "slaughter-pen" and tried to have the whole garrison withdrawn from the log rectangle with its unfinished back and sides. John Rutledge thought otherwise.

"General Lee still wishes you to abandon the fort," he wrote to Moultrie. "You will not do so without order from me. I would sooner cut off my hand than write one."

Sullivan's Island curves like a crooked finger. There is a small body of water between it and the mainland. Lee had a makeshift escape bridge laid across so that the defenders of the palmetto log "slaughter-pen" could escape. The bridge consisted of two planks laid across barrels that would float. So they did—with nobody on them. When a body of riflemen tried to cross, however, the planks sagged into the water and the riflemen had to wade ashore, wet to their waists.

On May 31, 1776, riders from up the coast brought news that the fleet had been sighted about twenty miles north of the harbor entrance. On June 1, the British appeared within sight of the town. Charles Town was a mass of confusion with horses and wagons taking families and baggage to the country, and militia marching into the town gates. Warehouses along the Cooper River that had cost their owners' life savings to build were torn down so that defensive guns could have free range. The streets were blocked with clever inventions to slow up the British if they should land. Apparently only John Rutledge, William Moultrie, and his men believed that the frail log fort would halt the fleet. Since there was a shortage of lead for bullets, the lead window-weights of private houses were ripped out and given for more ammunition.

Throughout this near panic, Moultrie remained unexcited. "I was never uneasy at not having a retreat," he wrote later, "because I never imagined that the enemy could force me to the necessity. I always considered myself able to defend that post against an enemy."

A general who simply could not imagine himself defeated!

Moultrie also remembered Thomson's riflemen stationed near Breach Inlet at the eastern end of Sullivan's Island and trusted them. These heroic crack shots have been largely ignored in the story of the Sullivan's Island victory. Lt. Col. William Thomson, of the Back Country, had recruited some of the finest riflemen in the state. They had fought the Loyalists with success and had gained much experience. Now, in the blazing summer heat on Sullivan's Island, they were waiting for the British attack. On June 11, troops from Virginia and North Carolina arrived. Moultrie's whole force consisted of 1,400 North Carolinians, 500 Virginians, 1,950 South Carolinians, 700 miltia from Charles Town, and 1,972 country militia. Not all of these were in the fort, which was built to contain about 1,000 men.

N.º 1. FORT SULLIVAN afterwards called FORT MOULTRIE in the unfinished State it was on the 28.ᵗʰ June 1776. the numbers opposite each cannon show the weight of ball they carried. Only the part of the Fort which is shaded was finished.

N.º 2. Sketch of a part of Sullivan's Island, the Fort, the Main, and the Shipping, during the Attack of the 28.ᵗʰ June 1776.

Moultrie had the gout. Lee peppered him with questions. Did he think he could hold the fort? "Yes, I think I can," Moultrie replied calmly. A visitor who had seen the fleet said, "Well, Colonel, what do you think of it now? . . . When those ships come to lay alongside of your fort, they will knock it down in half an hour." "Then . . . we will lay behind the ruins and prevent their men from landing," Moultrie replied.

The fort was critically short of powder. There have been differing accounts of just how much was on hand, but it seems clear that Moultrie had about enough, at first, to fire each cannon thirty times, and supply the riflemen with

*An old map showing the plan
for the battle of Sullivan's Island*

about twenty-five rounds of ammunition. A ship anchored
in the cove behind the fort sent three hundred pounds
during the fight, but it was not much help.

The British took their time about coming in. On June
4, the fleet anchored off Charles Town. On the fifth, it
made soundings of the harbor channels and laid down
buoys to guide it close to the town. On the ninth, Sir Henry
Clinton, the British commander, landed on Long Island
with about 2,500 men.

The plan was to wipe up Thomson's riflemen first, just
as the ships attacked the fort and then march through
Breach Inlet, which they thought to be only a few inches

deep at low tide. Actually it was much deeper and swirling with dangerous currents. Clinton's men were protected by an armed schooner and a fleet of smaller boats supposed to cover the redcoats' advance. The riflemen were in a small, makeshift fort with two cannon that none of the men knew how to fire. But their deadly musket balls raked the decks of the ships sent to protect the British infantry and drove them off, as well as holding Clinton's redcoats at bay across Breach Inlet.

Not all the fleet arrived at once. By June 15, plans for attacking Sullivan's Island were ready, but not until June 25 did the big, fifty-gun *Experiment* arrive. On June 28, the largest British fleet ever seen in American waters was anchored off Sullivan's Island—Admiral Sir Peter Parker's *Bristol* (50 guns), five 28-gun warships and a special bomb-ship, the *Thunder*, with eight mortars. Nine ships with 248 guns and unlimited powder and ammunition against Moultrie's frail log fort and 31 powder-starved cannon!

Springs on the British anchor cables kept the ships steady for the firing ahead. They also made sitting ducks of the fleet, since the ships could not move quickly out of Moultrie's cannon-range.

The first shells struck the fort—and sank harmlessly into the sand-backed palmetto logs. Bombs buried themselves harmlessly in a swampy place in the middle of the fort or in the surrounding sand. When Moultrie's cannon replied, slowly and by twos, the slaughter began.

Eight of Moultrie's officers served as gun pointers, aiming each cannon as though it were a hunting rifle. All were notable marksmen; it is not too much to say that eight men's precision fire defeated the British fleet.

Shortly, near panic struck the fleet. The decks of the *Bristol* ran red and were swept clear of men. Her captain lost an arm. Below decks on the *Bristol*, Lord William Campbell received a chest wound which killed him later.

William Jasper saving the Carolina flag

About seventy balls went through the *Bristol* alone. Seventy-four of her men were killed or wounded. The *Experiment* lost fifty-seven killed and thirty wounded. Her captain also lost an arm. Word had gone out inside the fort, "Mind the two fifty-gun ships!" Loss of life on the other ships was small, but damage to the ships themselves was serious.

And all this time, British balls were striking the fort's palmetto walls and being absorbed.

Moultrie's gunners ran short of powder and his guns stopped firing. The British thought the fort was preparing to surrender. Five Americans who had been taken prisoners from their ships, as the British moved south, later reported that when the cry arose on the *Bristol*, "The yankees have done firing!" a shout went up, "By God, we're glad of it, for we never had such a drubbing in our lives!"

A British ball cut down the new, dark blue crescent flag from one of the fort's bastions. Sergeant William Jasper, a Georgian who had joined Moultrie's men some time before, cried, "Colonel, don't let us fight without our flag!"

"How can you help it, when the staff is gone?" Moultrie shouted.

"I will replace it!" cried Jasper. Leaping over the wall, right into the enemy's fire, he rescued the flag and climbed back into the fort. Attaching the tattered banner to a cannon sponge-staff, he raised it on the bastion and gave three cheers before leaping down, unhurt. South Carolinians remember this as one of the greatest moments in their history.

Few men in the fort were killed or wounded. One, however, Sergeant M'Donald, got a body wound and managed to gasp, "Fight on, my brave boys! Don't let liberty die with me today!" A moment later, he was dead.

Watching anxiously from Charles Town, John Rutledge had seen the fort's cannon stop firing. Collecting more powder from heaven knew where, he rushed it across to Moultrie with a pencilled note:

> I send you 500 pounds of powder. You know our collection is not very great. HONOR and VICTORY, my good Sir, to you and our worthy countrymen with you.
> Yours,
> J. RUTLEDGE
> P.S. Do not make too free with your cannon. Cool, and do mischief.

By that time, Moultrie had lighted his corncob pipe, which he was always careful to put aside when General Lee showed up, propped his gouty leg at a comfortable angle, and had grog, a mixture of rum and water, served out in fire buckets to his sweating gunners.

Thomson's riflemen had mopped up the British. Lee, boating and galloping between Charles Town and the fort, so far forgot his former orders as to tell Moultrie that he was doing very well where he was, and could remain!

Towards dusk, the British ships drew off. Some Virginia and New England sailors, taken prisoner by the British on their way south, slipped overboard, joined the South Carolinians, and gave many details of the victory. From them, Moultrie first learned of the heavy British loss in killed and wounded. And the fort rang with laughter as the prisoners told how one well-aimed cannon ball had neatly removed the seat of Admiral Sir Peter Parker's white knee-breeches, leaving him lame and most embarrassed.

While Charles Town had watched the battle, a young Quaker, Daniel Latham, waited, with his fine race horse until victory was sure and then rode to Philadelphia, where the Continental Congress was still meeting. He arrived so quickly that many people did not believe the news he brought. However, some Philadelphia people knew him and assured others that Latham was a truthful man.

Moultrie always said that if his fort had had enough powder, the fleet could have been wiped out. On June 29, most of Charles Town went over to the fort to see that all was well and to congratulate its defenders. Rutledge offered Jasper an officer's commission, but the sergeant refused it, saying that he wasn't well-educated enough to be an officer. Rutledge then gave Jasper his own sword. A final count of the fort's losses showed that only twelve men had been killed and twenty-four wounded.

Grateful Charlestonians sent over big barrels of rum for punch. Gen. Charles Lee wrote to Congress that "no men ever did, and it is impossible ever can behave better." The nameless fort was given the name of its chief defender, Col. William Moultrie. Long after the battle, a white palmetto tree was added to the flag of South Carolina, in honor of the logs that had absorbed all the cannonballs the British could send against them. On July 20, the Continental Congress voted its thanks to Gen. Charles Lee, Col. Moultrie, Col. Thomson, and the men of their commands.

No British fleet would trouble Charles Town for three more years. After that, the state would be invaded, the city taken, and the further story of South Carolina under British conquest would be one of revenge and cruelty.

Mercifully, on that glad June day, Carolinians could not foresee that dark future. Battles and skirmishes during the Revolution would be fought on South Carolina soil. The savage march of Lt. Col. Banastre Tarleton through the Low Country plantations would lay a swathe or ruin over the land that fifty years would not erase. In Charles Town, men, young and old, and even young women suspected of sympathy to the American cause would be imprisoned in the damp, dark dungeon under the Exchange until they "took protection"—an oath of allegiance to the king. Patriots' property was seized while their wives and children starved. The state would also be torn with civil war, as Loyalists fought against men bent on independence. Brokenhearted people still loyal to King George would sacrifice all and leave the state forever, to die in exile. Old Acting Governor William Bull was one of these.

News of the Declaration of Independence reached Charles Town on August 5, 1776. A great procession of citizens, military bands, clergymen, and judges in their robes gathered at the Liberty Tree. After a prayer by Bishop William Percy, Major Bernard Elliott, one of Fort Moultrie's defenders, read the Declaration of Independence. The crowd cheered and there were cannon salutes.

South Carolina was free.

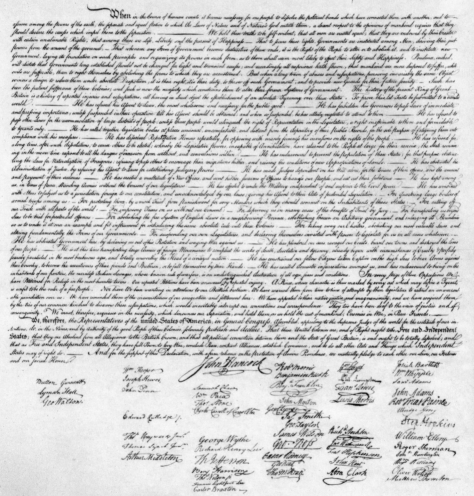

Edward Rutledge, Thomas Heyward, Jr., Thomas Lynch, Jr., and Arthur Middleton signed the Declaration of Independence in the second column

Bibliography

BARRY, R., *Mr. Rutledge of South Carolina*. New York: Duell, Sloan & Pearce, Inc., 1942.

CRANE, V. W., *The Southern Frontier, 1670–1732*. Durham, N. C.: Duke University Press, 1928.

LACHICOTTE, A. M., *Georgetown Rice Plantations*. Columbia, S. C.: State Printing Co., 1955.

MILLING, C. J., *Colonial South Carolina*. Columbia, S. C.: University of South Carolina Press, 1951.

MOULTRIE, W., *Memoirs of the American Revolution*. New York: New York Times and Arno Press, 1968.

PETIT, J. P., *Freedom's Four Square Miles*. Columbia, S. C.: R. L. Bryan Company, 1964.

POWES, F. B., *The Culture of Early Charleston*. Chapel Hill, N. C.: University of North Carolina Press, 1956.

QUATTLEBAUM, PAUL, *The Land Called Chicora*. Gainesville, Fla.: University of Florida Press, 1956.

RAVENEL, MRS. ST. J., *Charleston, the Place and the People*. New York: The Macmillan Company, 1929.

RHETT, R. G., *Charleston, An Epic of Carolina*. Richmond, Va.: Garrett & Massie, Inc., 1940.

SALLEY, A. S., *Narratives of Early Carolina*. New York: Charles Scribner's Sons, 1911.

SPRUILL, J. C., *Women's Life and Work in the Southern Colonies*. Chapel Hill: University of North Carolina Press, 1938.

STONEY, S. G., *Plantations of the Carolina Low Country*. Charleston, S. C.: Carolina Art Association, 1938.

WALSH, R., *Charleston's Sons of Liberty: A Study of the Artisans, 1763–1789*. Columbia, S. C.: University of South Carolina Press, 1959.

WRITERS PROGRAM, *South Carolina, A Guide to the Palmetto State*. New York: Oxford University Press, 1949.

Young people may especially enjoy the following books:

BEST, H., *Carolina Gold*. New York: John Day Co., 1961.

CARPENTER, A., *South Carolina*. Chicago: Children's Press, 1967.

FURMAN, M. S. O., *South Carolina from the Mountains to the Sea*. Columbia, S. C.: State Printing Co., 1964.

GRAYDON, N. S., *Eliza of Wappoo*. Columbia, S. C.: R. L. Bryan Co., 1968.

HENNIG, H. K., *Great South Carolinians*. Chapel Hill: University of North Carolina Press, 1940.

MAYRANT, D., *Always a River*. New York: Appleton-Century-Crofts, 1956.

MAYRANT, D., *Courage Is Not Given*. New York: Appleton-Century-Crofts, 1952.

MAYRANT, D., *The Red Doe*. New York: Appleton-Century-Crofts, 1953.

OLIPHANT, M. C. S., *The History of South Carolina*. River Forest, Ill.: Laidlaw Brothers, 1964.

ROGERS, F., *Indigo Treasure*. New York: Frederick A. Stokes, 1941.

Important Dates

1520—Captain Francisco Gordillo explores the Atlantic Coast.

1526—De Ayllón's first European settlement in eastern North America.

1540—De Soto explores South Carolina.

1562—Jean Ribault's Huguenot settlement on Parris Island.

1586—Spain gives up efforts to settle Carolina.

1629—Charles I grants "Carolana" to Sir Robert Heath.

1663—Charles II grants the same territory, renamed Carolina, to Lords Proprietors.

1670—First settlers land at Albemarle Point after stopping briefly at Port Royal.

1680—Charles Town moves across Ashley River to present site.
  —The coming of the Huguenots.

1706—French-Spanish attack on Charles Town.

1710-12—Provincial assembly passes free school law.

1711-12—South Carolina aids North Carolina in the Tuscarora War.

1715-17—Yamassee War almost wipes out South Carolina.

1715-18—Pirates threaten the province.

1719—Revolution against the Lords Proprietors.

1730—First royal governor, Robert Johnson, arrives.

1729—North and South Carolina officially divided.
  —System of townships established.

1731—Charles Town's newspaper, the *South-Carolina Gazette* founded.

1732-37—Townships settled.

1748—Parliament allows bounty on indigo raised in South Carolina—sixpence per pound. Wealth pours in.

1754—French and Indian War begins.

1760—Cherokee War begins.

1761—Cherokee War ends.

1765—Stamp Act passed.
  —Stamp Act Congress called.
1766—Stamp Act repealed.
1767—Townshend duties on glass, paper, lead, and tea.
1770—All taxes except tea tax removed.
  —Nonimportation of tea continues.
1773—Boston Tea Party.
1774—First delegates to First Continental Congress chosen.
  —The Charles Town Tea Party.
1775—Lord William Campbell dissolves the assembly, and provincial congress goes right on without him.
1776—March 26: South Carolina adopts her new Constitution and becomes an independent republic.
  —June 28: British fleet attacks Charles Town; Battle of Sullivan's Island.
  —July 4: The Declaration of Independence adopted.
  —August 2: The Declaration of Independence signed.

Places To Visit

Readers may wish to visit the following historical sites in South Carolina:

BEAUFORT St. Helena's Episcopal Church, founded in 1712, can be seen at Beaufort. Also Beaufort Arsenal, destroyed by the Yamassees in 1715 and later rebuilt. It is now a museum and relic room with artifacts dating from 1711. Monday through Friday, 10 A.M.–12 noon, 2 P.M.–4 P.M., except Wednesday morning. Free.

BETHANY Near here is King's Mountain National Park, scene of another American victory which prepared the British for the defeat at Yorktown.

CHARLESTON Here there are more than one thousand original buildings, many of them pre-Revolutionary. The Exchange at the foot of Broad Street, completed in 1771, was a Custom House. In March, 1776, the Provincial Congress established the first independent government in America at Charleston. In the Provost Dungeon, beneath the building, confiscated British tea was stored in 1773. The British established a prison for rebellious Carolinians after the fall of Charles Town. Part of the original town wall, now excavated, is here. Life-sized mannequins of men and women, some chained and watched by British sentries, show the terrible prison as it appeared during the British occupation. Daily, March 1–Labor Day, 9 A.M.–5 P.M., Monday through Saturday; Sunday, 12 noon–5 P.M.; Labor Day–February 28, 10 A.M.–2 P.M., Monday through Friday; Saturday, 10 A.M.–5 P.M. Adults, 75¢; children, 25¢.

The Charleston Museum is the oldest municipal museum in America. It holds a fine collection of Indian relics and dioramas; colonial interiors, furniture and costumes; pre-Revolutionary Charleston-made silver and pewter exhibits; tools from rice plantations. Free.

Old Powder Magazine, with walls thirty-two inches thick, is the oldest public building in Charleston, completed in 1713. It contains dresses woven of South Carolina silk, pictures, china and colonial furniture. Open Tuesday through Saturday, 9:30 A.M.–4:00 P.M., except in August. Adults, 50¢; children, 25¢.

The Bibbes Art Gallery has a fine collection of portraits of early Carolinians. Open Tuesday through Saturday, 10 A.M.–5 P.M. Closed Mondays and national holidays. Free.

The Heyward–Washington House, completely furnished in its period, was erected in 1770. It housed Washington when he visited the city in 1791 and contains magnificent Charleston-made furniture. Open 10 A.M.–5 P.M., Monday through Saturday. Adults, $1; children, 50¢.

The best time to visit the city and the Low Country is early March through April, when gardens throughout the city are a kaleidoscope of color. The Historic Charleston Foundation conducts a yearly series of historic house tours from March 21 through April 8, both in the daytime and at night when the homes are candlelit. Visitors walk through streets that have changed little in two hundred years. Tour prices range from $6–$7 and are open only to adults. There is a "Time Capsule Tour" (for children from seven to fourteen whose parents are on afternoon walking tours), which includes a bus trip to several historic landmarks and a tour of the U.S. Naval Base in the north area.

The Magnolia Gardens north of Charleston are world famous for azaleas and camellias. Open February 15 through May 1 from 8 A.M. to sundown. $2.50.

CLEMSON On the Clemson University campus is Hanover House, an original Huguenot dwelling. It was built in 1716 near the Sante River by Paul de St. Julien and was moved to Clemson when its original site was flooded by a power project dam. Restored and furnished in the style of its period, Hanover is unique among the state's historic houses. Open Wednesdays and Saturdays, 10 A.M.–5:30 P.M. Free.

COLUMBIA Museums of the colonial period include the Columbia Art Museum, with pictures by South Carolina artists, period furniture, Indian and Revolutionary relics, costumed dolls. Open Tuesdays, 10 A.M.–5 P.M.; Saturdays, 2 P.M.–6 P.M. Sundays. Free.

On the University of South Carolina campus is the South Caroliniana Library. The Kendall Memorial Room on the second floor contains rare maps, prints, books and so forth, dating from the early days of the state. Open September through May, Monday through Saturady, 9 A.M.—5 P.M.; June through August, Monday through Friday, 9 A.M.–5 P.M.; Saturday, 9 A.M.–1 P.M. Free.

COWPENS The scene of one of the decisive battles of the Revolution. Here, in 1780, 940 Continentals under General Morgan defeated 1,500 British regulars under Colonel Banastre Tarleton.

GEORGETOWN Site of the first European settlement on the North American continent in 1526, the town was founded in 1735. Many colonial structures are here, perhaps the most notable being the Episcopal Church of Prince George, Winyah, erected 1742–46.

LEXINGTON The Corley Museum is at the residence of Dr. G. L. Corley. It houses a fascinating collection of pottery, tools, guns and other artifacts of early Lexington County. Open Saturdays 10 A.M.– 4 P.M. and by appointment other days. Free.

MAYFIELDS Four miles northwest of Aiken are three buildings filled with Indian and early American exhibits. Open year round by appointment. Free.

PICKENS At the Pickens County Historical Museum are relics of early Up-Country life—Indian artifacts, pioneer tools and utensils, old guns and so forth. Monday, 2 P.M.–5 P.M. Free.

SPARTANBURG The regional museum here includes Indian and pioneer relics, Revolutionary General Daniel Morgan display and the Pardo Stone, with a carved date, 1567. It is completely furnished with many interesting out-buildings. Open year round, Tuesday through Saturday, 11 A.M.–4 P.M.; Sunday, 2 P.M.–5 P.M. Closed Monday. Adults, $1; students and children under 18, 50¢.

Times and admission prices
are subject to change.

Index